WOMAN
IN
MUSLIM SOCIETY

WOMAN
IN
MUSLIM SOCIETY

N . M. SHAIKH

KITAB BHAVAN
New Delhi-110002

Kitab Bhavan
Publishers, Distributors, Exporters & Importers
1784, Kalan Mahal, Darya Ganj
New Delhi - 1100 02 (India)

Phone : (91-11) 23277392/93, 23274686, 30906494
website : www.kitabbhavan.com
Email : nasri@vsnl.com
Fax : (91-11) 23263383

First Edition 1991
IInd Reprinted 2005

ISBN : 81-7151-131-7
Code No. : W00047

Published in India by :
Nusrat Ali Nasri for Kitab Bhavan
1784, Kalan Mahal, Darya Ganj
New Delhi - 1100 02 [India]

Printed in India at :
Nice Printing Press
Khureji Khas, Delhi-110051

WOMAN IN MUSLIM SOCIETY

CONTENTS

†-†-†-†-†-†-†-†-†-†-†-†-†-†-†-†-†-†

بسم الله الرحمن الرحيم

CHAPTER 1

WOMEN IN DIFFERENT COUNTRIES IN ANCIENT TIMES

The journey of mankind began with the union of man and woman. It also spread the human race and evolved science and art, trade and industry and civilization and culture.

All other relations amongst mankind are either the outcome of the union of man and woman or are the result of external causes and circumstances in the absence of which no such relations could be evolved. A neighbour loves another neighbour, a companion embraces another companion, a traveller joins another traveller; similarly a student associates with another student and a trader cooperates with another trader, because they have mutual interest. But as soon as their interests cease, they fall apart and become strangers to each other. But this is not the case with the union of man and woman. Their union is based on the natural feeling and attraction which keep them united in spite of their range of action and interest being quite separate.

A woman, no doubt, nurtures the human race with her blood and looks after the affairs of her home, but she finds it difficult to work in the field and defend herself against the enemies, for, she has no sufficient strength to do so. Her heart is the abode of only love, sympathy and sacrifice; whereas man is hard and sturdy, therefore, his duties include hunting, farming, trade and defence.

This difference of strength between man and woman has been the matter of grace and disgrace in periods of history. Man has physical power and strength; what he can do, a woman cannot do because of natural weakness, so man was considered superior and woman inferior. Hence, the countries which were well-known for their justice, character-building and grant of human rights, considered man as superior to woman.

Woman in Greece and Rome

We have, to some extent, detailed knowledge of ancient history of the Greeks and the Romans. Their culture, civilization and knowledge of science and arts considerably flourished so much so that on their bases many cultures came into being. But in spite of all these, the place of woman was very low in their societies. They would regard her only a burden on human being. Her only purpose was to serve man in the house like a maid servant.

In spite of all their lofty ideas and rationalism, the Greeks had very ridiculous concepts about women. They would say :

> "There is a cure for burning by fire and snake-bite but there is no cure for a woman's mischief."

She had to live under the subjugation of her parents in childhood, of her husband in youth and of her children in widowhood. On the other hand the rights of her male relatives were always superior. Though the law provided her with the right of divorce but practically, it was of no avail because the act of going to court of law was considered a matter of shame and disgrace in the Greek society. No doubt Plato pleaded for the equal rights for man and woman but this was no more than a theoretical preaching and was nowhere in practice. The purpose of marriage was just political, that is, to produce strong and healthy children for the defence of the country. It was laid down in the law of Sparta that, the husbands who were not fully young or weak, should offer their young wives to healthier and stronger young man to enable them produce sturdy soldiers for the army.

The Roman Law kept the status of woman very low for a long time. The head of the family, either or husband, had full authority over his wife and children. He could turn out his wife at any time he wanted. There was no system of dowry. The father had the right to give her daughter in marriage to anybody at his sweet will. He could also break the marriage. Later on, this right was transferred to the husband who could even kill his wife if he so desired. The system of divorce was unknown for about 520 years.

In Roman society, the purpose of woman was like that of slaves. Man used to marry woman only for his own benefit. She was never considered fit for any post or even able to give evidence in any matter. She had no legal rights whatsoever; only some facilities were granted to her because of her physical weakness. Of course, woman was given some rights by the Romans in later period, yet she was not treated equal to man.

> When if one of them receiveth tidings of the birth of a female, his face remaineth darkened, and he is wroth inwardly. (16 : 58)

Woman in Arabia before Islam

Woman was thought as a cause of disgrace and shame in ancient Arabia. The birth of a daughter would make the Arabs sorrowful and sad. They would feel pride in having sons but felt ashamed of having daughters. The Holy Quran has perfectly described their feelings in this regard.

> "When one of them receiveth tidings of the birth of a female (daughter), his face remaineth darkened, and he is wroth inwardly. He hideth himself from the folk because of the evil of that whereof he hath had tidings, (asking himself): Shall he keep it in contempt or bury it beneath the dust. Verily evil is their Judgment",
> (16 : 58-59).

The Holy Quran further depicts the feeling of the father of the Age of Ignorance in respect of the news of the birth of a daughter in these words :

> "And if one of them hath tidings of that which he

likeneth to the Beneficent One, his countenance becometh black and he is full of inward rage." (43 : 17)

Thus, before the advent of Islam, a large number of Arab fathers buried their newly born daughters alive in order to escape their whimsical and superstitious disgrace.

Moreover, they had no feeling of kindness and love for woman, and they buried their daughters alive. A man related his own action during the days of ignorance to the Holy Prophet Muhammad (S.A.W.) :

"I had a little daughter who loved me very much. Whenever I called her, she came running happily towards me. One day I called her, as usual she came running and then followed me. I took her to a nearby well and pushed her in. At that moment she cried, "Father, father." The Prophet of Islam (S.A.W.) was shocked to hear it and his eyes were filled with tears." *(Sunan Darimi)*

It is stated that Qais bin 'Asim had buried alive about eight daughters during the days of *Jahiliya*.

(Tafseer Ibn Kaseer)

Even if the Arabs kept their daughters alive, they deprived them of all their rights. There was no limitation for marriage. They married as many women as they liked. When Wahab Asadi (R.A.A.) embraced Islam, he had ten wives.

(Abu Dawood)

Similarly Gheelan Saqfee also had ten wives at the time of his conversion to Islam. *(Tirmizi)*

Likewise, there were no restrictions on divorce, man was free to divorce his wife any time and any number of time and reunite at will. *(Mustadrak)*

The wife had to serve her husband during his life-time and after his death, his heirs had full rights over her. They were free to marry their step-mothers themselves or got her married with anyone they liked. They were also authorised to prevent her from marrying anyone. In order to misappropriate the wealth and property of the widow, they did not allow her to re-marry. If she were a minor, her marriage was delayed, so that they may marry her themselves.

Allama Abu Bakr Jassas writes :

"It was a common practice to marry step-mothers during the days of ignorance". *(Ahkamul Quran)*

Whenever, an Arab happened to be the guardian of a pretty and wealthy girl, he would himself marry her and paid no dower. *(Bukhari).*

In pre-Islamic Arabia, woman had no right of inheritance. After the Battle of *Uhud*, the wife of Sabit bin Qais complained to the Holy Prophet (S.A.W.) that her husband had been martyred and she had two daughters. But Sabit's brother had misappropriated everything. Now, how would she arrange for their marriage ?" *(Abu Dawood).*

When Islam granted woman the right of inheritance, the Arabs were wonder struck and asked the Prophet of Islam (S.A.W.), "O Prophet of Allah! how can a woman inherit half of the property when she cannot ride a horse nor defend herself?" *(Tafseer Ibn Kaseer)*

Woman in Europe

In modern world, Europe claims to have given all the rights to woman. But the same woman was the victim of man a century ago and there was no law to prevent a male from tyrannizing the woman. The husband had full right over the wealth and property of his wife. There was no law of maintenance of wife. She could not sue her husband. He could even deprive his wife of her right to property.

Woman was not free to deal in any matter whatsoever. She had no right to sign any contract. She was neither allowed to spend money earned by her nor to marry a man of her choice.

Daughters were the property of their parents. Marriage was nothing but a trade because they used to sell their daughters to whomsoever they liked.

Before the advent of Christianity, man was the master of woman. There were no rules and regulations for the control of a man. Even after Christianity, woman has no equal rights. At the time of nuptial she is asked to swear before the priest to remain obedient to her husband for whole of her life in all circumstances. She can do nothing without his permission. She has no right to own her property because it automatically becomes the property of her husband. Thus her position is worse than a slave.

CHAPTER 2

WOMAN IN DIFFERENT RELIGIONS

Woman in Judaism

The concept of Judaism about woman is that she is frail and vicious. She is an image of deceit. In order to support this dictum, the Jews relate the story of Hazrat Adam and Eve. According to them, the Prophet Adam (A.S.) lived happily in the Heaven because he was obedient to Allah. But his wife, Eve, incited him to eat the forbidden fruit and thus disobeyed Allah. Consequently Adam (A.S.) was deprived of all bounties of Allah and was expelled from the Heaven to suffer.

According to the Old Testament, Allah questioned Adam, "Did you eat the fruit forbidden by me?" Adam replied, "The woman who Thee gave me, offered me the fruit and I ate it." Then Allah said to Eve, "We shall aggravate the pain of your child-bearing. You will give birth to babies painfully. You will always be inclined to your husband and he will rule over you." Thus Allah punished Eve for inciting Adam to disobey Him and established the authority of man over woman for ever. Hence woman had to be obedient to man until the Day of Judgment. According to Jewish Law, woman is deprived of the right of inheritance in the presence of male heir. She had no right to marry second time in her life.

> "And I find more bitter than death the woman, whose heart is snares and nets, and her hands as bands; whoso pleaseth God shall escape from her; but the Sinner shall be taken by her." *(Old Testament)*

Woman in Christianity

The attitude of Christianity towards woman has been still worse. According to father Tertulian (A.D. 150) a woman opens the door to Satanic temptations, leads man to the forbidden tree, breaks the law of Allah and corrupts man-the image of God.

> "She is the gate through which the devil enters, She is the beguiler of man to the forbideen tree, She is the breaker of the Law of God and is the plunderer of man, who is the image of God."

Another exponent of Christianity named Chrysostom remarks about woman :

> "She is an inevitable evil, a born whisperer of evil, an amiable affliction, a domestic danger, a plundering allurement and an embellished misfortune."

In a letter St. Paul writes :

> "Woman must learn the art of obedience quietly. I would not allow woman to teach or govern man. On the contrary, she must remain silent. Adam was created first and then Eve. Not Adam, but Eve was deceived and committed sin." *(St. Paul first letter to Tymothus)*

In another letter he said that every man's head was Christ, every woman's head was man and Christ's head was God. Man was the countenance and glory of God but woman was the glory of man; not because man was dependent upon woman, but because woman was dependent upon man. Man was not born for woman but woman was born for man. Hence, for angel's sake, she must consider herself to be the symbol of slavery. (St. Paul's first letter to Tymothus) Thus we see that in modern Christianity the status of woman is that of a slave.

Woman in Hinduism

In Hinduism also, woman is a slave. A famous Indian legislator, Manoo Raj has said, "woman in her childhood must remain under the custody of her father, in youth she must remain under the custody of her husband and when widowed she must remain under the custody of her sons. She must never be independent. Woman, whether minor or young or old, must not act independently in the house. It is sin for woman to offer sacrifice or fast. Her duty is only to serve her husband and in case of his death she must never think of second husband. She must eat less, so pass rest of her life. To tell lies is the nature of woman." (vide Manu Samarti articles 5/145, 5/147, 5/155. 5/157 and 9/17, quoted in *Nizam-e-Saltanat*, by Akber Shah Khan *Najeebaa-di).*

Another Hindu scholar, Chanakya says, "River, armed soldier, animals with horns and paws, king and woman must not be trusted. Telling lies, acting without thinking, foolishness, greed, unholiness and mercilessness are the instinctive defects in woman. You can learn manners from the princes, politenss from scholars, falsehood from gamblers and wickedness from woman. Fire, water, ignorance, snake, royal family and woman are the cause of destruction; therefore, beware of them. Friend, servant and woman shun the company of a poor man, they come back to him when he becomes rich again." (vide articles 1/15,2, 12/18, 14/12 and 14/5 of Chanakya Niti as quoted by *Nizam-e-Saltant* by Akber Shah Khan *Najeebaadi),*

The custom of *Sati* in India is a clear proof of the fact that there is no independent existence for woman in Hindu society. She is deprived of her right even to live after the death of her husband.

CHAPTER 3

WOMAN AND MODERN AGE

Woman was victimised for a long time. When her agony reached its climax, the situation became very serious. The modern age brought revolution in every aspect of life and changed the status of woman. Formerly she was slave but now she is 'free'. The Industrial Revolution in Europe helped woman achieve her 'Freedom'. She broke the chain of 'slavery' and came in the open field. The doors of employment were opened for her which helped her to revolt against man.

Woman desired freedom not for the betterment of her lot but for vengeance. She went to such an extent in this process that she herself took the place of man. She forgot the fundamental principle that woman can't take the place of man. Both are quite different in their capabilities and characteristics. Man and woman are physically and psychologically quite different from each other.

The main difference between man and woman is of sex and this difference cannot be removed by means of education, training or environment. They differ in their very nature. What a man can do, a woman cannot do it; and what a woman can do, a man cannot do. But the West accepted the equality of man and woman not because it has proved their natural differences wrong but simply because it found it the only solution for the freedom of woman from 'man's tyranny'.

It is explicitly clear that the West has created its own standard of respectability. According to this criteria, only the characteristics and strength of man have been taken into consideration and the nature of woman has been neglected. She has been invited to bring herself to that standard if she wants to be honourable in the society. In fact, she ought to have been assigned the task according to her nature and capabilities. Then, she would have not resorted to the artificial means to acquire dignified position in the society.

The Western thinkers maintain that present concept of the nature of woman is nothing but an artificial state created by man's constant tyranny. Her talents have been suppressed. Had she been free to act, she would have achieved better position even in the fields reserved for man.

As far as intellect and reasoning are concerned, it is wrong to say that man and woman are equal in these respects. They think woman would have performed her duty better if she had been free to act. But it is also possible that she would have remained at the same position where she was before, despite her freedom to act. Hence it is false to say that she can also fulfil the responsibilities of man.

The history shows that woman had opportunities, in different periods, to struggle along with man, but she failed to achieve the status of man owing to her natural weaknesses. Besides, the modern world has provided her freedom along with man for over the last one century, but her freedom has brought no change of any sort in her feminine nature.

Another stand that Western thinkers take, is that if woman is removed from civil and social work, the advancement in the field of modernization would be reduced to fifty percent and the progress of fifty years will take one full century. This argument is absolutely false and baseless, as society is not a technical institution for the progress of one particular technique. On the contrary, it came into existence due to the association of various departments of human life. Some of these departments belong to woman also. If these departments are abolished, the whole society will suffer. Hence, evolution of society means progress of every department to achieve overall higher standard of life.

Despite all facilities, woman has not been proved as useful as expected in the assigned fields. A less qualified man has been proved more useful than a highly qualified woman. The reason is that woman wants to do the work of man but her nature does not allow her to succeed in her efforts. Her natural characteristics forbid her to follow the modern trend. This struggle has put her in such a condition that worries even the West.

It is a proven fact that Western way of living has failed to provide a dignified status to woman in the society.

CHAPTER 4

WOMAN IN ISLAMIC SOCIETY

Human Dignity

The sum total of Islamic teachings is to raise human dignity and honour. It relieves mankind from disgrace and provides higher and honourable place in human society. It imparts the lesson of human dignity. Islam directs humanity to prostrate before Allah alone for the achievement of superiority over other creations. Mankind is the masterpiece creation of Allah. The following verses of the Holy Quran testify this fact :

> Verily We have honoured the children of Adam. We carry them on the land and the sea, and have made provision of good things for them, and We have preferred them above many of those whom We created with a marked preferment. (17 : 70)

> Surely We created man of the best stature. (95 : 4)

> "When thy Lord said unto the angels : Lo : I am about to create a mortal out of mire. And when I have fashioned him and breathed into him of My spirit, then fall down before him prostrate. The angels fell down prostrate, everyone save *Iblis*; He was scornful and became one of the disbelievers." (38 : 72-75)

Standard of Superiority—Faith and Practice

In Islam the welfare of mankind depends upon right thinking and right practice. It is sheer ignorance to degrade woman simply because she happens to be a woman, and man is considered heavenly creature simply because he happens to be a man. Islam has explained it in very clear words that human dignity rests upon piety and virtue. Hence, who is more honourable, man or woman? This question is well answered by the Holy Quran :

> "Whosoever doeth right whether male or female, and is a believer, him verily We shall quicken with good life and We shall pay them recompense in proportion to the best of what they used to do." (16 : 97)

> "Lo! Men who surrender unto Allah, and women who surrender, and men who believe and women who believe, men who obey and women who obey, and men who speak the truth and women who speak the truth, and men who persevere (in righteousness) and women who persevere, and men who are humble, and women who are humble, and men who give alms, and women who give alms, and men who fast, and women who fast, and men who guard their modesty, and women who guard (their modesty), and men who remember Allah much and women who remember Allah hath prepared for them forgiveness and a vast reward." (33 : 35)

> "And their Lord hath heard them (and He saith): Lo! I suffer not the work of any worker, male or female, to be lost. Ye proceed one from another. So those who migrated and were driven forth from their homes and suffered damage for My cause and fought and were slain, verily I shall remit their evil deeds from them and verily I shall bring them into gardens underneath which rivers—flow a reward from Allah, and with Allah is the fairest of rewards." (3 : 195)

The Holy Quran distinctly explains the characteristics of the *Momineen* (The faithful followers of Islam) who submitted their lives, property and desires to the Will of Allah :

> "(Triumphant) are those who turn repentant (To Allah), those who serve (Him), those who praise (Him), those who fast, those who bow down, those who fall prostrate

(in worship), those who enjoin the right and who forbid the wrong, and those who keep the limits (Ordained) of Allaḥ, and give glad-tidings to believers!" (9 : 12).

At another place, the pious wives of the Holy Prophet (S.A.W.) have been commanded to develop such qualities in them without which they would not be able to remain in his *Nikah.* And the Holy Prophet (S.A.W.) would easily find such wives who would possess such virtuous qualities.

"It may happen that his Lord, if he divorces you, will give him in your stead wives better than you, submissive (to Allah) believing, pious, penitent, inclined to fasting, widows and maids." (66 :5)

Now, it becomes crystal clear that according to the Holy Quran, piety and virtue are the only criteria for the achievement of successful life in the Hereafter. None, whether man or woman can accomplish his or her goal without fulfilling this condition.

Man And Woman : The Architects of Civilization

The Holy Quran points out that man and woman both have helped and cooperated with each other in the development of human life. Both have equally shared the burden of life. Their union has brought the civilization into existence. No nation or movement of the world can neglect either of them. If man and woman are responsible for the establishment of the authority of Truth and its enforcement, they are equally responsible for the spread of vices in the world. The Holy Quran says :

"The hypocrites, both man and woman, are one and the same. They enjoin the evil, and forbid the right; and they withhold their hands from spending in the cause of Allah. They have forgotten Allah and so He hath forgotten them. Indeed, the hypocrites, are the transgressors." (9 : 76)

"And the believers, men and women are protecting friends one of another; they enjoin the right and forbid the wrong, and they establish the prayer and they pay the poor-due, and they obey Allah and His Messenger, as for these, Allah will have mercy on them. Lo! Allah is Mighty Wise." (9 : 71)

Since it is admitted that the revolutions in the civilization of the world are brought about by both, man and woman, no logical argument can degrade one and upgrade the other. Besides, it will be foolish to eliminate either of them from the civilization and march forward. No person can play any role in life after having paralysed one half of the body.

The Islamic View of Woman

Before the advent of Islam, the world had degraded the woman and had almost outcast her. She was thrown in such deep abyss that there seemed no hope of her redemption. Islam boldly remonstrated against this injustice and emphasised that life needed both man and woman. Woman is not created to be derided and cast aside. Like man, woman also has her purpose and right to exist. And the Nature is achieving its aim with the help of man and woman both. As the Holy Quran says :

Unto Allah belongeth the Sovereignty of the heavens and the earth. He createth what He wills. He bestoweth female (offsprings) upon whom He will, and bestoweth male (offspring) upon whom He will; or He mingleth them, males and females, and He maketh barren whom He will. Lo ! He is Knower, Powerful. (42 : 49-50)

Islam lifted woman from the abyss of disgrace and granted her rights and facilities. Abdullah-bin-'Umar (R.A.A.) relates :

During the life time of our Prophet, Muhammad (S.A.W.) we did not talk to our woman freely because we feared revelation against us. When the Holy Prophet (S.A.W.) passed away, we became frank with them.

(Bukhari, and Ibn Majah)

Whereas, all other religions deprived woman of right even to live. Islam granted her rights almost at par with man. It also warned that all those who strive to snatch her rights away, will surely be accountable to Allah on the Day of Judgment.

And when the girl-child that was buried alive, is asked : For what sin she was slain ? (19 : 8-9)

The Holy Prophet (S.A.W.) has issued numerous instructions in favour of woman, the favour which she could not receive even from the so-called modern upholders of the woman's rights. The Holy Prophet (S.A.W.) has said :

Allah has forbidden you, disobedience unto your mothers, refusal to sanctioned rights, accumulation of wealth from all sides and burial of living daughters. *(Bukhari)*

The Prophet of Islam (S.A.W.) has also said :

"A man who has a duaghter and he neither despises her nor buries her alive nor prefers son to daughter, Allah will admit him in Heaven." *(Abu Daud)*

Abu Sayeed (R.A.A.) relates that the Holy Prophet (S.A.W.) said :

"Whoever brought up three daughters and treated them well, the Heaven is for him." *(Abu Daud — Tirmizi)*

The world condemned woman, but Islam honoured her. The Holy Prophet (S.A.W.) raised her status and assigned her respectable place in the human society. He (S.A.W.) said :

"In worldly things, I like woman and perfume, but coolness of my eyes lies in *salat* (Prayers)".

Once the Holy wives were travelling on camels, the Holy Prophet (S.A.W.) said to the camel driver.

"Carry these glasses very carefully."

About Fatimah (R.A.A.) the Messenger of Allah (S.A.W.) has said :

"My daughter is my flesh, any trouble to her will cause pain to me." *(Bukhari, and Muslim)*

Once Hazrat Aisha (R.A.A.) was asked whom did the Holy Prophet (S.A.W.) loved most? She replied, Fatimah (R.A.A.).

On another occasion, somebody asked the Holy Prophet (S.A.W.), 'Who is your most beloved person?" The Holy Prophet (S.A.W.) replied, ' Aisha (R.A.A.)."

Thus we see that the Holy Prophet (S.A.W.) loved his wife Aisha (R.A.A.) and his daughter Fatima (R.A.A.) most. And the sayings of the Holy Prophet (S.A.W.) explicitly explain the aim of Islam with regard to the treatment of fair sex.

The teachings of Islam revolutionized the thinking of those men who buried their daughters alive and felt no shame in doing so. They began to love and nourish their daughters, those who refused to shelter their own daughters, became the guardians of other's daughters. Those who were devoid of love and affection for women, now loved and cared for them.

On the occasion of the Battle of *Uhud*, Jabir's father told Jabir (R.A.A.), "My Son! I may be martyred in the forthcoming battle, so I advise you to look after my daughters." Consequently, Jabir (R.A.A.) who was still young, married a widow owing to the responsibility of his sisters. The Holy Prophet (S.A.W.) asked him, "Why did you not marry a young woman?" He replied, "O Prophet of Allah (S.A.W.) ! My father was martyred in the Battle of *Uhud* and he has left behind his nine daughters who are my sisters. Therefore, I chose such woman for my marriage, who could look after them well." The Messenger of Allah (S.A.W.) replied, You did a good deed." *(Bukhari)*

It is related that after the martyrdom of Hazrat Hamza (R.A.A.), three persons claimed to have the right to look

after his daughter. The first was Hazrat Ali (R.A.A.) who claimed his right to look after her because she was his cousin (sister). The second person was Hazrat Jafer (R.A.A.) who said that his claim was better than that of Hazrat Ali (R.A.A.) because she was not only his cousin (sister) but her maternal aunt was his wife. Hence, she could be brought up in better way. The third man was Hazrat Zaid (R.A.A.) who filed his petition on the ground that she was his brother's daughter and that none else can have better claim than her own uncle.
(Bukhari, and Muslim)

These are the examples which the history of other nations cannot present. Islam is the only religion that raised the status of woman to such extent in the world.

Equality in Rights

According to Islam, society is responsible for the protection of human rights and maintenance of law and order. Its duty is to chop off the hands of the oppressors and unjust. The Quran says :

> "And there is life for you in retaliation, O men of understanding, that ye may ward off (evil)." (2 : 179)

The law of *Shariah* awards death penalty to murderer whether he has murdered a man or a woman, because the life of woman is as sacred as that of man. The laws given to the people of Yaman by the Holy Prophet (S.A.W.) included the death penalty to the murderer of woman also.

> "Undoubtedly (men) murderer of a woman shall be sentenced to death."

It is stated that a Jew crushed the head of a girl and killed her. The Holy Prophet (S.A.W.) ordered him to be put to death in the same manner *(Bukhari and Muslim)*

Once, all those men who murdered a woman, were put to death by the order of Hazrat 'Umar Farooq (R.A.A.)
(Al-Ahkam-ul-Quran, Jassas)

If a woman pardons a murderer of her relative, the other relatives have no authority to nullify her consent for forgiveness. Not only this, she can offer protection to an enemy during the emergency of war and this act of her cannot be considered unlawful. The Holy Prophet (S.A.W.) has said :

> "Undoubtely, a woman can shelter an enemy for the benefit of Muslims." *(Tirmizi)*

On the occasion of the conquest of Holy Mecca, Umm Hani said to the Holy Prophet (S.A.W.), "O Messenger of Allah (S.A.W.), I have provided protection to Ibn Hera, but Ali (R.A.A.) says that he will kill him under any circumstance."

The Holy Prophet (S.A.W.) replied, "Umm Hani ! Whomsoever you have protected, he is under my protection too." *(Bukhari)*

Similarly, Islam permits woman, within the limits of *Shariah*, to participate in the financial affairs and derive benefits.

No man can interfere in this matter. Even her husband has no right to make use of her personal wealth. Likewise, woman has no right to enforce her will for the use of the wealth of her husband. There is a distinct injunction of the Holy Quran :

> "And covet not the thing in which Allah hath made some of you excel other. Upto men a fortune from that which they have earned and unto women a fortune from that which they have earned. (Envy not one another). But ask Allah of His bounty. Lo ! Allah is Ever Knower of all things." (4 : 32)

According to the Holy Quran the Law of Inheritance is :

> "Unto the men (of a family) belongeth a share of that which parents and near kindred leave, and unto the women a share of that which parents and near kindred leave, whether it be little or much a legal share." (4 : 7)

The Common Law

The ancient religions were not prepared to give equal status to man and woman. Therefore, they formulated separate laws for them. But Islam does not make this distinction. In Islam, man and woman both are equal before law. The Holy Quran says :

> "Lo ! We offered the trust unto the heavens and the earth and the hills, but they shrunk from bearing it and were afraid of it. And man assumed it. Lo ! He hath proved a tyrant and a fool. So Allah punisheth hypocritical men and hypocritical women, and idolator men and idolator women. But Allah pardoneth believing men and believing women, and Allah is Forgiving, Merciful." (33 : 72-73)

> "And it becometh not a believing man or a believing woman when Allah and His Messenger have decided an affair (for them), that they should (after that) claiming say in their affair, and whoso is rebellious to Allah and His Messenger, he verily goeth astray in error manifest." (33 : 36)

The Law of Spouses

Islam has granted equal rights to both, man and woman. It provides equal opportunity to both of them for the progress and prosperity of life. It guanantees the protection of their lives, property and honour.

The spouses are equally inter-dependent. Therefore, there is no question of honour for man and dishonour for woman. In Islam both are equally honourable. There is no distinction on the basis of sex. In fact they are created for each other to live in harmony and co-existence. As the Holy Quran says :

> "They are raiment for you and ye are raiment for them." (2 : 187)

The relation between man and woman is not of hatred but of love. Man is incomplete without woman and woman is incomplete without man. They are the source of peace and harmony to each other.

According to the Holy Quran :

"And of His signs is this : He created for you help-mates from yourselves that ye might find rest in them, and he ordained between you love and mercy. Lo ! herein indeed are portents for folk who reflect." (30 : 21)

CHAPTER 5

REAL FIELD OF WOMAN IN ISLAM

Addressing the Holy wives of the Holy Prophet of Islam (S.A.W.), the Holy Quran has said :

> And stay in your houses. Do not exhibit your decorations as in the Days of Ignorance. Be regular in prayer and pay the poor-due and obey Allah and His Messenger, Allah's Will is but to remove uncleanliness far from you, O Folk of the household and cleans you with a thorough cleansing. (33 : 33)

After the Hijrat (Migration from Mecca to Madina), the Holy Prophet (S.A.W.) and his companions were struggling to make Madina a model of Islamic virtues. What they could not establish in Mecca, they wished to do in Madina. But the evil forces were adversely creating hindrance in their way. As soon as the Holy Prophet (S.A.W.) launched his movement to establish Islamic way of life in Madina, the evil forces also raised their heads against him. Within the period of six years, the opposition grew so strong that they felt as if the truth will vanish and evil forces will rule forever.

The disturbance created by the hypocrites engulfed the whole city of Madina. The opponents were striving to uproot the plants of morality and righteousness from the surface of Madina. They wanted total annihilation of piety and virtue therefrom. Their main targets were the honour of men and chastity of women. They knew that without toppling this basic principle, they would not be able to satisfy their carnal desires.

Under the circumstances, Islam formulated new laws for the protection of the country and the nation. It ordered Muslim men to fight face to face and crush the evil forces. It also allowed women to participate in the battle but within the limits of their houses. Hence, it is crystal clear that Islam has assigned the task of protecting the state and the society to men and confined the struggle of women to their own houses.

If a woman leaves her actual place—home, it creates a gap which cannot be filled by anyone else. Therefore, Islam has not made incumbent upon women to participate in congregational prayers and such other prescribed duties of life.

It is incumbent upon man to offer his prayers in congregation. Prayer is also incumbent upon woman but not necessarily in congregation. If man tries to avoid congregation without any valid reason, he is subjected to warning and chastisement. Whereas, woman is encouraged to offer her prayers at home. They Holy Prophet (S.A.W.) has said :

> "The best mosques for women are the inner parts of their houses." *(Musnad Ahmad)*

Once the wife of a well known companion of the Holy Prophet, (S.A.W.) Abu Humaid Saa'di (R.A.A.) came to the Holy Prophet (S.A.W.) and said, "O Messenger of Allah (S.A.W.) . . . I wish to offer my prayers alongwith you in the mosque. What is your opinion?" The Holy Prophet (S.A.W.) replied, "I know that it is your desire, but remember, it is better for you to offer your prayers in the inner room of your house rather than to offer your prayers in the outer room of your house. The prayer which you offer in your room is better than the prayer which you offer in the courtyard of your house, and the prayer which you offer in the courtyard of your house is better than the prayer which you offer in the mosque of your locality. Similarly, the prayer which you offer in the mosque of your locality, is better than your prayer which you offer in my mosque." *(Musad Ahmad)*

The wife of Abu Humaid Saaidi (R.A.A.) was so much impressed by the order of the Holy Prophet (S.A.W.) that she selected a corner of her room and prayed there until the end of her life.

Friday is the manifestation of congregation and the unity of the Muslim nation. But the woman has been exempted from offering Friday prayer in the mosque. The Holy Prophet (S.A.W.) has said :

> "Friday prayer is incumbent upon every Muslim except- slave, woman, child and the sick." *(Abu Dawood)*

Holy Prophet Muhammad (S.A.W.) has also disapproved the participation of woman in the funeral. In this respect Umme Atiya (R.A.A.) relates : "We were prevented from taking part in the funeral procession but the Holy Prophet (S.A.W.) was not so strict with us." This *Hadis* shows that the Holy Prophet (S.A.W.) was not so strict but another *Hadis* shows that he (S.A.W.) was strict in a sense.

Hazrat Anas (R.A.A.) relates, "Once we were accompanying the Holy Prophet (S.A.W.) in a funeral procession. He (S.A.W.) saw some women following and asked angrily, "Are you carrying the dead body?" They replied, No. The Holy Propnet again asked : "Will you particpate in the burial?" They replied, "No." The Holy Prophet (S.A.W.) said, "When you have nothing to do here, why have you come? You will get nothing in return, so go home."

(Fath-ul-Bari)

It is also not incumbent upon women to take part in *Jihad* (Holy War) and come to the battle field. In such delicate situations also, they have been advised to remain within the four walls of their houses and serve the cause of Islam in the best possible way. Hazrat Ayesha (R.A.A.) relates that the Holy Prophet (S.A.W.) has said, "You (women) should remain within the four walls of your homes (i.e. look after domestic chores) and this is your *Jihad.*"

(Musnad Ahmad)

Once a *Sahabia* (Female Companion) asked the Holy Prophet (S.A.W.), "Allah has made *Jihad* incumbent upon men, so when they return victorious, they share the booty and if they are martyred, they live eternally and Allah provides them with their livelihood. But which action of ours will be equivalent to theirs ?"

The Holy Prophet (S.A.W.) replied, "Obedience to your husbands and the recognition of their rights."

(Al Targheeb wal Tarheeb)

Thus we see that in Islam duties of man and woman are different but the reward is the same. In no case the equal right of woman is lost. She can come out but for the welfare of her home and not for its destruction. Hazrat Ayesha (R.A.A.) asked the Holy Prophet (S.A.W.), "Is *Jihad* incumbent upon women ?" The Holy Prophet (S.A.W.) replied, "Yes, *Jihad* is obligatory for them but in that *Jihad*, there is no war and that is *Hajj* and *Umra*". *(Ibn Majah)*

In reply to another question he (S.A.W.) remarked, "*Hajj* is the best *Jihad* for you (women)." *(Bukhari)*

Women are allowed to offer their prayers in the mosque on the condition that they do not mingle with men and keep their rows separate. Hazrat Abu Hurairah relates that the Holy Prophet (S.A.W.) has said :

> "The best row of men is the first row and the worst is their last row. And the best row of women is the last and the worst is their first row." *(Muslim)*

The Islamic Society Is One Unit

Apparently we see the functioning of different organiza tion differently but in fact these organizations and institutions are the parts of the one single social set-up. A body of government runs the affairs of the country; the judiciary deals with justice the municipalities look after the civic affairs of the cities; schools, colleges, and universities impart education, and commercial organizations manage the trade and industries of the country. But all these organizations are governed by one social set-up.

Though Islam has confined the place of woman to her home, she has not been deprived of her right to participate in other organizational activities. On the contrary, Islamic society makes her a useful member of the society. She can acquire education and become specialist in her own field. She can become a doctor and treat women and children. She can become a teacher and impart education to women folk. In short, she can participate in all activities of the society and choose her career within the limits of the Islamic Laws.

Islam builds human character and aims at the establishment of a society free from all vices and immoralities, Hence woman prevented from indulging in such activities which become the cause of social degeneration. Umme Atiya relates, the Holy Prophet (S.A.W.) has said :

"The minor and the major women and those women who are pregnant may go to *Idgah* (Place of *Eid* prayers). But those women who are in menses will keept away from the place of prayer and participate only in supplications.

CHAPTER 6

EDUCATION OF WOMAN

Background

Before the advent of Islam, Arabs were groping in the darkness of ignorance. There was no importance of life for them. Their main aim was to acquire more and more material progress for worldly pleasure. The realities of life were beyond the range of their thinking.

Islam, explained to them the real philosophy of life and provided the complete code which included moral restrictions and the principles of right and wrong. It gave them the clear concept of Heaven and Hell. It taught them to obey Allah and His Messenger, Muhammad (S.A.W.)

When these Arabs gradually accepted the teachings of Islam, a new society came into existence. It was refined and free from all vices. During the evolution of Islamic Society, a commandment of Allah was revealed :

> "O Prophet, if believing women come unto thee, taking oath of allegiance unto thee that they will ascribe nothing as partner unto Allah, and will neither steal nor commit adultery nor kill their children, nor produce any lie that they have devised between their hands and feet, nor disobey thee in what is right, then accept their allegiance and ask Allah to forgive them. Lo ! Allah is Forgiving, Merciful." (60 : 12)

In this verse of the Holy Quran, woman has been directed to follow certain principles of Islam. However, it becomes essential for woman to educate herself in order to understand

and follow the principles in letter and spirit. She has been categorically instructed to obey the Holy Prophet (S.A.W.). This commandment made women to think and seek the knowledge of Islamic teachings. The Muslim women practised the principles of Islam and acquired honourable status in the society. Hazrat Ayeshah (R.A.A.) says :

> "The Ansar women were wonderful ! Nothing could check them from understanding of Islam." *(Muslim)*

The women during the times of the Holy Prophet (S.A.W.), acquired profound knowledge of teachings. Hazrat Ayesha (R.A.A.) says :

> "We used to memorise, not only but injunctions of every verse of the Holy Quran revealed to the Holy Prophet (S.A.W.). *(Al Iqdul Farid)*

Responsibility of Parents

The real place of woman's education is her home. Therefore, Islamic *Shariah* directs the parents to educate their daughters so that they may be able to distinguish between right and wrong. It is the duty of the parents to educate their daughters in order to provide them an honourable status in the society. Without education, it is not possible for a woman to understand the teachings of Islam and mould her life accordingly. The Holy Prophet (S.A.W.) has encouraged the education of women and thus earn the pleasure of Allah, in these words :

> "Whosoever brought up three daughters, taught them manners and etiquette, got them married and treated them well, Haven is for him." *(Abu Dawood)*

Duty of Husband

The foundations, of the family in Islam are blood ties and marital obligations. No other type of relationship, like "Adoption" "Mutual Alliance", "Common Law", "Trial

Marriage" or "Mutual Consent" to sexual intimacy, will constitute family in the Islamic sense. Islam appreciates the religious virtues, the social necessity and the moral advantages of marriage. There are many verses in the Holy Quran and sayings of the Holy Prophet (S.A.W.) which go as far as to say that when a Muslim marries, he has thereby perfected half of his religion; so let him be conscious of these religious obligations and be careful with the other half.

There are many statements of the Holy Quran and traditions of the Holy Prophet (S.A.W.) that prescribe kindness and equity, compassion and love, sympathy and consideration, patience and goodwill. The Holy Prophet (S.A.W.) goes as far as to declare that the best Muslim is the one who is best to his family, and the greatest, most blessed joy in life is a good and virtuous wife.

These ethical principles allocate to the wife certain rights and corresponding duties. It is the husband's duty to behave with his wife in an equitable and kind manner. He is bound for the full and adequate maintenance of his wife, a duty which he must discharge cheerfully, without reproach, injury, or bickering.

The Holy Quran says :

> "O ye who believe ! Ward off from yourselves and your families a fire whereof the fuel is men and stones, over which are set angels strong, severe, who resist not Allah in that which He commandeth them, but do that which they are commanded." (66 : 6)

Malik-bin-Huvairis says that he, alongwith some other youngmen, stayed with the Holy Prophet (S.A.W.) for twenty days to acquire the knowledge of Islam. When he (S.A.W.) realized that we were anxious to go home, he (S.A.W.) said, "Go to your wives and children and live with them and teach them the principles of Islam and order them to practise." *(Bukhari)*

Hazrat 'Umar Farooq (R.A.A.) wrote to the people of Koofa "teach them *Surah Noor.*"

The Holy Prophet (S.A.W.) said, "There are three types of men who will be rewarded twice as such. One of them is that man who has a maid and teaches her good manners and imparts her better education and after freeing marries her." *(Bukhari)*

Once, the Holy Prophet (S.A.W.) got a woman married to a very poor man. The Holy Prophet (S.A.W.) asked him to teach the *Surah* of the Holy Quran that he knew to his wife in lieu of dower. *(Bukhari)*

Sometime, the Holy Prophet (S.A.W.) instructed the men to teach particular portions of the Holy Quran to their wives. For instance, he (S.A.W.) said, "Undoubtedly, Allah has completed *Surah Baqarah* (The Cow) with two verses which have been given to me from the treasure which is under Heaven. So you learn and teach them to your wives also." *(Darimi)*

A daughter of the Holy Prophet (S.A.W.) says that while teaching her, the Holy Prophet (S.A.W.) used to say, "When you rise in the morning say that Allah is Holy and that He alone can provide the power to praise Him. Whatever Allah wishes it happens and whatever He wishes not, it happens not. Remember, Allah commands everything and He is the Knower of everything." *(Abu Dawood)*

Woman's Legal Rights

The well-known Maliki scholar and jurist Allama Ibn Alhaj has written :

> "If woman demands her right in respect of *Deen* (Islam) from her husband and approaches the ruler of the time for the issuance of an injunction in her favour for the acquisition of religious education which is her legal right, that is, either the husband himself should educate

her or allow her to go out and study, then it is obligatory upon that ruler to order her husband to fulfil her wishes, as he (The ruler) does in case of worldly rights. Because the religious rights are more important than the material." *(Al Mudkhal Ibn Alhaj)*

Imam Fakhruddin Hasan Bin Mansoor Hanafi (d. 295 A.H.) in his famous *fatwa*, says, "A woman has no right to participate in any literary sitting without the prior permission of her husband, when any problem arises, she should consult her husband. If the husband is not a learned man, he should solve the problem with the help of other learned men, then she must not leave her house without his permission. However, if the husband fails to make research and solve her problem, then she can visit any educational institution without his permission and get the problem solved. Because it is incumbent upon both, man and woman, to acquire knowledge. Specially, when the wife is helpless, her right to acquire knowledge will have priority over the husband's right." *(Fatawa Qazi Khan)*

The Result of Educational Facilities for Woman

Islamic *Shariah* provides all facilities to woman to acquire knowledge. It intends to develop her mental powers in order to become a useful member of the society. Islam emancipated woman from ignorance and made her position dignified and honourable. 'Urwah bin Zubair, (R.A.A.) says about Hazrat Ayeshah (R.A.A.) :

"Hazrat Ayeshah (R.A.A.) knew more about the injunctions of Holy Quran, poetry and literature, the History of Arabs and their heirarchy than any other person."

Moosa bin Talha says :

"I have not come across any other person more eloquent than Hazrat Ayeshah (R.A.A.)." *(Tirmizi)*

Ibn Abee Malkah (R.A.A.) asked Hazrat Ayeshah (R.A.A.), "We are not much surprised by your knowledge of prose and poetry because you are the daughter of Hazrat Abu Bakr Siddique (R.A.A.) whose literary status is well-known. But from where did you learn the medical science?" She replied, "Whenever the Holy Prophet (S.A.W.) fell sick, the medical team prescribed medicines for him. I learn the use of these medicines from them."

Hazrat Ayeshah was so apt in accounts that the senior companions of the Holy Prophet (S.A.W.) used to consult her on matters of inheritance.

Umrah bint Abdur Rahman was one of the students of Hazrat Ayeshah (R.A.A.) . Ahmad Ibn Hambal says about her, "The Jurist, Umrah bint Abdur Rahman was brought up by Hazrat Ayeshah (R.A.A.). She related a great number of *hadis* through her which are authentic. Her memory is sharp." "Ibn Hibban testifies about her, "She has learnt most of the *hadis* from Hazrat Ayeshah."

Allama Ibn Abdul Birr (R.A.) says about Hazrat Zainab (R.A.A.), "She was a great jurist of her time."

Abu Rafay Sa'igh says, "When I talk of any woman jurist of Madina, I at once remember Zainab bint Abi Salma."

Ummul Hassan, a maid of Hazrat Umme Salamah (R.A.A.) was a great scholar who preached and delivered sermons to women.

About Ummul Momineen Hazrat Safiyah, Imam Navavi says, "She was one of the wise and intelletual women."

It is said that Fatima bint Qais (R.A.A.) argued with Hazrat 'Umar (R.A.A.) and Hazrat Ayeshah (R.A.A.) over a juristic problem for a long time but they could not change her view. The other scholars also gave preference to her thought. Imam Navavi has said about her, "She was one of those who migrated in the earlier period and was a versatile genius."

Hafsa Bint Seerin (R.A.A.) of Basrah completed the study of the Holy Qur'an when she was just twelve years old. The famous Judge of Basrah, Ayas-bin-Muawiya says about her;

"I did not come across any other person whom I could give superiority over Hafsa Bint Seerin."

(Tahzib-al-Tahzib)

Sayeed bin Musayyab had married his daughter to his pupil. The next day her husband was preparing to attend the literary sitting of her father. She said to him, "Be at home, what Sayeed bin Musayyab can teach you there, I can teach you here."

Similarly, the daughter of Imam Malik (R.A.) was a learned lady. If a student made a mistake while reading *Moatta*, she used to knock at the door of her room from inside. Imam Malik had full confidence in her knowledge, therefore, he used to ask the erring student to repeat it correctly.

About Umme Varaqa Bint Naufil (R.A.A.), it has been said, "She had studied the Holy Quran, therefore, the Holy Prophet (S.A.W.) had allowed her to lead the prayers of the female members of her family."

A famous Maliki Imam, Ash'hab (R.A.) once bought some vegetables from a maid. In those days it was a custom to give bread to the seller in lieu of money. Ash'hab (R.A.) had no loaf at that time. Therefore, he asked the maid to come and collect the loaf from him in the evening when he would get it from the baker. She replied that it was not fair because according to the *Shariah*, the exchange of commodities must take place on the spot." *(Al-Mudkhal, Ibn Alhaj)*

The history shows that most of the Muslim women not only knew reading but they were well versed in writing as well. They were competent to write letters and note down various problems.

Woman's Contribution to Education

Educated Muslim women made great contribution to the cause of education and learning. They became the source of guidance and enlightement for the society. Imam Ibn Qayyim says :

"The Companions of the Holy Prophet (S.A.W.) who were competent to issue religious decrees *(fatwas)* were about one hundred and thirty. This number includes men and women both." The persons who issued most of the *Fatwa* included Hazrat Ayesha (R.A.A.) and Hazrat Umme Salama (R.A.A.).

The other women who issued few *Fatwa* are :

Umme Atiya, Hazrat Hafsa, Hazrat Umm Habiba, Hazrat Safiya, Laila bint Qaiyim, Asma bint Abi Bakr, Umme Sharik, Khaula bint Towait, Umm Darda, Atika bint Zaid, Sahla bint Hazrat Juwairia, Hazrat Maimoona, Hazrat Fatima bint Qais, Hazrat Umme Salama, Zainab bint Umm Salama, Umm Aiman, Umme Yusuf and Ghamadiya (R.A.A.).

These wise and learned women made a great contribution to the cause of Islamic teachings and helped in the uplift of the society.

Hazrat Ayesha (R.A.A.) was a renowned scholar of *Ahadis*. She has narrated two thousand, two hundred and ten *Ahadis*. Her knowledge was so apt that sometimes she corrected Hazrat 'Umar (R.A.A.) and Abu Hurairah (R.A.A.) Hafiz Ibn Hajar says :

"Hazrat Ayesha (R.A.A.) had learnt a great many things from the Holy Prophet (S.A.W.) and lived for fifty years after him (S.A.W.). People were greatly benefitted by her. Many principles were related through her and it is said that one-fourth of the laws of *Shariah* were related by her."

Suhairah bint Huzair has said about Hazrat Safiyah (R.A.A.), "I, alongwith some other women, went to Madina after Hajj and visited Hazrat Safiyah (R.A.A.). There were already some women from Koofa. We requested her to explain to us the laws regarding the relation of husband and wife and other relevant topics."

The knowledge of the Holy wives of the Holy Prophet (S.A.W.) greatly helped in the solution of the problems which puzzled the Companions of the Holy Prophet (S.A.W.). Imam

Ibn Qaiyim (R.A.) says : "When there was any difference of opinion amongst the Companions of the Holy Prophet (S.A.W.) and any of the *Ummahatul Momineen* quoted any *hadis*, then they accepted it and forgot their differences."

(Zadul M'aad Vol. 4, Page-221)

About Umme Atiya (R.A.A.), Allama ibn Abdul Bir (R.A.) has said : "She attended the after-death bathing ritual of the daughter of Holy Prophet (S.A.W.) and she explained the principles of bath *(Ghusl)* very efficiently. Her *hadis* regarding bathing of dead body has become the fundamental principle (for Muslims). The Companions of the Holy Prophet (S.A.W.) and their disciples in Basrah learnt the rules of the bathing of the dead body from her; and there are many other *Ahadis* also, which have been related through her by Ans-bin-Malik, Muhammad bin Seereen and Hafsa bint Seereen."

(Al Istiab)

CHAPTER 7

WOMAN IN PRACTICAL LIFE

Woman Is Allowed to Go out for Good Cause

Islam wants woman to be able and efficient, so that she may preform good deeds and serve mankind. Hence, she is allowed to go out for the attainment of good cause. The study of history shows that woman went for shopping and farm-work during the early period of Islam. Hazrat Ayesha (R.A.A.) relates an incident which took place just after the revelation of Commandments of veil. She says, "When Hazrat 'Umar Farooq (R.A.A.) once saw Hazrat Sauda (R.A.A.) outside her house, and expressed his displeasure on this. She came away quietly and related the matter to the Holy Prophet (S.A.W.). Soon after there was revelation upon him (S.A.W.). When it was over, the Holy Prophet (S.A.W.) told her :

> "Of course, Allah has permitted you to go out of your home for your needs." *(Bukhari)*

There are such other instances which show that Islamic Society never prevented women from going out of their homes for the right cause and necessary requirements.

"But Islam has laid down certain limitations on the movements of woman. Whenever she leaves home and goes out, she has to remain within the protective bounds of her modesty and chastity. She is not permitted to move so freely and mingle with men in social gatherings.

Going of Woman to Mosque for Prayers

Woman is allowed to visit mosque for the purpose of offering her prayers. However, this permission is not without conditions. The Holy Prophet (S.A.W.) has said :

> "When a wife of one of you asks for permission to go to mosque, she should not be refused."
>
> *(Muslim, and Bukhari)*

But men were not directed, either to send women or bring them along to mosque. Hazrat 'Umar Farooq (R.A.A.) did not like his wife Aliqah going to mosque for offering her prayers. Whenever she asked for the permission, he kept quiet. And she herself would reply, "By Allah, I shall go to mosque to offer my prayers unless I am prohibitted in clear terms." *(Mu'atta)*

The woman who went to mosque to offer her prayers, was neither allowed to mix with men in the congregation nor stand in the front rows. There is a clear direction of the Holy Prophet (S.A.W.) in this respect.

"The best place for women is at the rear."

Whether Woman is Allowed to Join Funeral Procession and Visit Graves

Hazrat Umme Atiyah (R.A.A.) relates, "We were prohibited, though not strictly, from accompanying funeral processions." *(Bukhari)*

Once a woman, who happened to be the close relative of the deceased, accompanied his funeral procession owing to the grief beyond her control. Hazrat 'Umar Farooq (R.A.A.) reproved her but the Holy Prophet (S.A.W.) remarked, "O 'Umar ! leave her alone."

Similarly, the Holy Prophet (S.A.W.) prohibited the frequenting of the graves by woman. Hazrat Anas Bin Malik

(R.A.A.) relates, "When the Holy Prophet (S.A.W.) saw a woman crying over a grave, he (S.A.W.) did not prevent her, but advised her, "O woman ! Fear Allah and have patience."

(Bukhari)

Woman's Travelling

A Muslim woman, whether spinster, married or widow, can not travel alone. She can travel only in the company of a *mahram* (a relative with whom her marriage is prohibited).

"It is unlawful for a woman who believes in Allah and the Day of Judgment to travel for three days or more without accompanying either her father, brother or husband or son or any other male *mahram.*"

Further, Hazrat Abu Hurairah (R.A.A.) relates that the Holy Prophet (S.A.W.) has said :

"A woman should not travel for a day and night unless she is accompanied by a male *mahram.*" *(Abu Dawood)*

Woman in The Field of Trade and Commerce

Woman can carry on any lawful business or trade, without restriction of any kind. According to Islamic Shariah. the conception of a state is of a welfare state, in which woman also plays an important role. We have various examples.

A *Sahabia* named Qeela (R.A.A.) said to the Holy Prophet (S.A.W.), "I am a woman who buys and sells different commodities and want to know the principles of trade."

(Tabaqat Ibn Sa'd)

During the Caliphate of Hazrat 'Umar Farooq, Abdullah bin Abi Rabiya used to send *'Itr'* (scent) to his mother Asma from Yaman and she carried on its business.

Umrah bint Tabeekh says, "Once I went to the market alongwith a maid and bought fish and put it in the bag. As the bag was small, its head and tail were visible. Hazrat Ali

(R.A.A.) who was passing from there, saw the fish and asked, 'How much did you pay for it? It's very big and nice. All members of the family would eat with satisfaction."

(Tabaqat Ibn Sa'd)

Woman in Agriculture

Woman is also free to go on her farm and work there. Jabir bin Abdullah (R.A.A.) says that his aunt was divorced by her husband. She decided to cut and sell a few trees during the period of her *Iddat* (waiting period). A gentleman told her that she was not allowed to leave her home during the period of her *Iddat.* So she went to the Holy Prophet (S.A.W.) to seek his advice. The Holy Prophet (S.A.W.) said :

"Go on to your field, cut your date trees and sell. You may give the earned money in charity or use it for some other good purpose and thus you may be rewarded in the Hereafter." *(Abu Dawood)*

Sohail bin Sa'd (R.A.A.) relates the story of another woman who had her own farm where she cultivated beet-roots. When he alongwith other companions visited her on Fridays, she would entertain them with a sweet dish made from beet-root and flour. *(Bukhari)*

Hazrat Abu Bakr Siddiq's daughter Asma (R.A.A.) says: "The Holy Prophet (S.A.W.) had given a piece of land for cultivation to Hazrat Zubair (her husband) which was at a distance of two miles from my house. I used to bring date-stones from that farm. Once when I was carrying a basket, full of date stones on my head, I met the Holy Prophet (S.A.W.) on the way. He (S.A.W.) called me and offered a place at the back of his mount. But as there were some Ansar males with him so I felt shy to travel with them. I also thought of my husband, Hazrat Zubair (R.A.A.) who was a very self respecting man and would have never liked it. Realizing my hesitation, the Holy Prophet (S.A.W.) proceeded on."

Woman in Industry

Woman participated in industrial activities also. Hazrat Abdullah bin Mas'ood's wife ran an industry very successfully and supported her husband and children through its income.

Similarly, Khaula Bint Sa'lba (R.A.A.) earned through the industrial work and maintained her husband also.

(Tabaqat Ibn Sa'd, Vol. 8)

Woman's Right of Freedom

Islam provides full protection to the rights of woman. The rights granted to her by Islamic *Shariah* cannot be taken away by any man. Whenever their rights were encroached upon by anyone, they defended it to their best.

Once a man married his daughter to a rich man. The girl did not like him so she complained to the Holy Prophet (S.A.W.), and said, "My father has married me to his wealthy nephew so that he may get some benefits."

The Holy Prophet (S.A.W.) replied, "If you do not like this marriage, then you are free." She submitted, "I uphold my father's decision. By this complaint I intended to tell my fellow women that their fathers have no right to marry them against their will. *(Musnad Ahmad)*

A slave maid, Barera (R.A.A.) was married to a slave man named Mughees (R.A.A.). After sometime, she became free then she refused to live with Mughees (R.A.A.) as a free woman was not legally bound to remain in the wedlock of a slave man. But Mughees (R.A.A.) loved Barera (R.A.A.) so much that he became desperate and used to follow her weeping. Seeing his miserable state the Holy Prophet (S.A.W.) said to her :

"Barerah! Fear Allah and and think of the love and anxiety of Mughees. He has been your husband so long, and you have borne his children as well."

Barerah (R.A.A.) asked, "Are you (S.A.W.) ordering me to remain his wife ?"

The Holy Prophet (S.A.W.) replied, "No, how can I order you? I am just recommending his case to you."

She said, "Then I do not need him." *(Bukhari)*

During the time of the Holy Prophet (S.A.W.), women offered prayers in mosque. Due to some reasons Hazrat 'Umar Farooq (R.A.A.) felt that it was not advisable for women to leave their homes and move out. As they had been permitted by the Holy Prophet (S.A.W.), he did not like to restrict them by force of law.

Hazrat 'Umar Farooq's own wife, 'Ateka (R.A.A.) availed the advantage of the permission and offered her prayers in congregation. Once he told her, "By Allah, you know I don't like this practice of yours, and yet you do not desist." She replied: "By Allah, I shall continue to offer my prayers in mosque unless you prevent me by law. "Thus, she did not stop praying in the mosque during the lifetime of Hazrat 'Umar Farooq (R.A.A.), so much so that she was present in the mosque when the murderous attack was made on him. *(Bukhari).* This event proves that women's rights are fully safeguarded in the Islamic society.

Once the Holy wives of the Holy Prophet (S.A.W.) demanded from him some amenities of life. As such demand was below their dignity and status and also did not conform to the way of life he (S.A.W.) liked, hence he was very much displeased and he decided not to talk to them for one month. When Hazrat Abu Bakr Siddiq (R.A.A.) and Hazrat 'Umar Farooq (R.A.A.) came to know, they felt it very much. They told their daughters, Hazrat Ayesha (R.A.A.) and Hazrat Hafsa (R.A.A.) that their demand was not fair. Likewise, they endeavoured to explain their views to other wives of the Holy Prophet (S.A.W.). Finally they went to Hazrat Umme Salama (R.A.A.) who told them :

"Gentlemen! What is your business here? The Holy Prophet (S.A.W.) is well aware of our position. If he (S.A.W.) wants, may prevent us, then we shall not claim anything. To whom should we approach except him? Does anybody interfere in the affairs between you and your wives? You may leave, we have not invited you."

(Tabaqat Ibn Sa'd Vol. 8)

It is crystal clear that Hazrat Umme Salama (R.A.A.) would not like even such important personalities to intere-fere in her domestic affairs. She wanted that the dispute between wife and husband should be settled between them only and nobody else should be allowed to interfere.

CHAPTER 8

WOMAN'S CONTRIBUTION TO THE ISLAMIC SOCIETY

The Sacrifices of the Muslim Women

The Muslim women have made great sacrifices for the cause of Islam. They faced all the difficulties of life and remained firm. No power on earth could shake their faith.

The family of Ammar-bin-Yasir (R.A.A.) had embraced Islam in the early period of prophethood at Mecca. His mother was a slave of Abu Huzaifa-bin-Mughairah and was tortured for having embraced Islam. So much so that she was speared to death by Abu Jah'l. She died and became the first martyr in the cause of Islam but did not leave Islam.

Hazrat 'Umar Farooq (R.A.A.) was still a non-Muslim when his sister Fatima (R.A.A.) embraced Islam. He beat her severely, but this battering could not weaken her faith. She always replied him boldly, "O son of Khattab ! I have become a Muslim. You may beat me any way you like, but I will never change my faith." When seeing her steadfastness Hazrat 'Umar Farooq (R.A.A.) wanted to see that wonderful Book the Holy Qur'an, she boldly replied, "O son of Khattab ! Do not touch it because you are unclean and only clean person can touch this sacred Book." *(Mustadrak Hakim)*

There is another similar event. When Abu Sufian was still a non-Muslim he visited Madina to see the Holy Prophet (S.A.W.). He also went to see his daughter, *Ummul Momineen* Umm Habiba (R.A.A.) who was Holy Prophet's wife. He was going to sit on the bed of Holy Prophet (S.A.W.) but his daughter removed it. The father got annoyed and asked, "Do you think I am not fit to sit on this bed ?" The daughter replied, "This bed belongs to the Holy Prophet (S.A.W.). You are a non-believer and infidel, hence I cannot allow you to sit on it." *(Tabaqat Ibn S'ad)*

There is a clear injunction of the Holy Qur'an that Muslims should have no relation with the enemies of Allah. Once the infidel mother of Hazrat Asma (R.A.A.) came to her house at Madina from Mecca and brought gifts with her. Before admitting her in the house, Hazrat Asma (R.A.A.) enquired from the Holy Prophet (S.A.W.) whether she could admit her in the house and treat her with honour and sympathy. The Holy Prophet (S.A.W.) replied, "Yes, you can."

Ruqiqah bint Abee Saifi (R.A.A.) had embraced Islam during a very dangerous period. She was the lady who informed the Holy Prophet (S.A.W.) that the Quraish of Mecca were planning to assassinate him. Therefore, the Holy Prophet (S.A.W.) migrated to Madina that night for his safety.

Women's Role in War

Though it is not obligatory upon women to participate in *Jihad*, they came forward at critical times of War and fought side by side their men-folk against the enemies of Islam.

An Ansari *Sahabia*, Umme Ammara (R.A.A.) showed manly and daring courage during the battle of *Uhud*. She herself relates : "I had reached the battlefield early in the morning to serve *Mujahideen* (The warriors of Islam). In the beginning the Muslims were winning but the whole affair was disturbed later on. I went very close to the Holy Prophet (S.A.W.) and fought with sword in hand to defend him. I was wounded." Seeing the serious wounds on her shoulders Umme Sa'd (R.A.A.) asked her, "Who attacked you so severely?" She replied, "Ibne Qamia, curse of Allah be upon him ! When a large number of Muslims ran away he came to me and said, "Tell me, where is Muhammad (S.A.W.) ? If he

(S.A.W.) escapes, I shall be destroyed." When I heard him, I along with Musab bin Umair (R.A.A.) and others who were with the Holy Prophet (S.A.W.), fought with him and he attacked me, I also attacked him vigorously but he had worn two armours (so escaped)." The Holy Prophet (S.A.W.) himself praised her in these words :

> "Left or right, in whichever direction I looked, I found Umme Ammara defending me." *(Seerat Ibn Hisham)*

An enemy wounded her son. When he passed by, the Holy Prophet (S.A.W.) said, "Umme Ammara, this is the man who has wounded your son." Hearing this, she attacked him with her sword and he fell on the ground. The Holy Prophet (S.A.W.) smiled and said, "Umme Ammara, you have avenged your son." After that they continued their attack until the time the war was over. The Holy Prophet (S.A.W.) said, "Thanks to Allah, Who gave you strength to overpower him, coolness to your eyes and enabled you to revenge your son."

Relating another incident, Umme Ammara (R.A.A.) says, "A horse-rider came forward and attacked me. I defended myself with the help of my shield. When he turned his back in order to escape, I attacked him with my sword and chopped his legs and he fell on the ground. The Holy Prophet (S.A.W.) who was watching this event, called my son for my help. He came running to me and I killed the enemy with his help."

Besides *Uhud*, Umme Ammara (R.A.A.) had taken part in the battles of *Khaibar*, *Hunain* and *Yamama*. On the day of *Yamama*, she lost her hand and received twelve serious wounds of swords and spears. *(Tabaqat)*

Umme Hakeem (R.A.A.), the wife of Ikrama (R.A.A.) bin Abu Jahl participated in the battle between the Muslims and the Romans. Ikrama was martyred in the battle of *Ajnadeen*. After some days she married Khalid-bin-Sayeed (R.A.A.) at *Maraje Safar*. Next day was the *Valeema* (Wedding Dinner). The Romans launched attacks before the dinner party was over. When the battle started, she took a stick and killed at least seven enemies with it. *(Istiab)*

Asma Bint Yazeed killed nine Romans in the battle of *Yarmook.*

When the Muslim army was losing its ground in the battle of *Hunain*, Umme Haris (R.A.A.) alongwith a few brave soldiers, faced the enemies like a rock.

During a battle, a well known warrior, Habib-bin-Salam's wife asked him, "Tell me ! Where will you be tomorrow ?" He replied, "Inshah Allah (God Willing), I shall be either on the battle-field or in Paradise." She said, "Wherever you may be, I shall be with you." *(Al Bayan wal Tibyan)*

At the time of the battle of Ditch *(Khandaq)*, the Holy Prophet (S.A.W.) left women in the fort so that they may remain comparatively safe. But the Jews kept an eye on the fort. One of them got an opportunity and climbed the wall of the fort. The aunt of the Holy Prophet (S.A.W.), Hazrat Safiya (R.A.A.) who was in the fort, came forward and slew him and threw his dead body down where the other enemies were waiting. They were wonder struck and said, "Muhammad (S.A.W.) would not leave the women unguarded in the fort. Certainly, there would be some selected warriors in the fort to frustrate our designs." *(Mustadrak Hakim)*

Women have played greater role by indirect participation in wars. They helped the archers and the swordsmen on battle-fields. They nursed the wounded soldiers and provided water and food to the needy persons. Rabi Bint Muawwoz (R.A.A.) says : "We participated in *Jihad* along with the Holy Prophet (S.A.W.). We used to give water to the *Mujahideen* and helped in carrying the wounded and the martyred soldiers to Madina. *(Bukhari)*

Umm Atiya (R.A.A.) says about herself :

"I participated in seven battles along with the Holy Prophet (S.A.W.). There I took care of the belongings of the *Mujahideen*, prepared food for them and attended the sick and the wounded." *(Muslim)*

Tabarani Relates :

"When the infidels returned after the battle of *Uhud*, the women went to help and nurse the companions of the Holy Prophet (S.A.W.), Hazrat Fatima was one of them. When the Holy Prophet (S.A.W.) was wounded, she filled his wound with the mat-ash." *(Bukhari)*

Hazrat Anas (R.A.A.) relates that Hazrat Ayeshah (R.A.A.) and Umme Sulaim (R.A.A.)had also served the *Mujahideen.* He says : "I saw Hazrat Ayeshah Bint Abu Bakr and Umme Sulaim (R.A.A.) serving the people. They carried water bags on their back and quenched the thirst of the soldiers. They performed this duty briskly and repeatedly." *(Bukhari)*

Hazrat 'Umar Farooq (R.A.A.) relates about an Ansari lady Umme Saleet (R.A.A.) :

"She used to bring bags full of water for us on the day of *Uhud.*" *(Bukhari)*

Hamna Bint Jahsh also performed the same duty on the day of *Uhud.* Ibn Sa'd has written. "She was present on the day of *Uhud;* she gave water to the thirsty and treated the wounded." *(Tabaqat-al-Kabir)*

It is related about Umm Ammara (R.A.A.) :

"She had left for the battle-field early in the morning for the purpose of helping the wounded and supplying water to the thirsty. Her son says that she carried the bandage rolls for treatment of the wounded, she bandaged my wounds also."

The historian, Ibn Ishaq says : "Many women participated in the battle of *Khaiber* along with the Holy Prophet (S.A.W.)."

The grandmother of Hashraj Bin Ziyad and other five women also participated in the battle of *Khaiber.* They related the purpose of their arrival to the Holy Prophet (S.A.W.) in these words :

> "O Messenger of Allah (S.A.W.), we have come to help in the way of Allah. We have medicines for the wounded. We shall provide arrows to the archers and prepare *sattoo* (a preparation of flour) for the soldiers."
>
> *(Abu Dawood)*

Hazrat Rafeeda (R.A.A.) had established a camp hospital in a tent near the *Masjid-e-Nabavi* and treated the wounded soldiers. When Hazrat Sa'd-bin-Muaz was wounded in the battle of *Khandaq*, he was brought to the same hospital so that he may be properly looked after by her. *(Istiab)*

Not only women participated in battles directly and indirectly, but also encouraged others to fight in defence of Islam and Muslims.

After embracing Islam, Urwa bint Abdul Muttalib (R.A.A.) the aunt of the Holy Prophet (S.A.W.) helped him and encouraged her son to carry on the mission of Islam. Her son, Taleeb (R.A.A.) had embraced Islam in the early period of the Holy Mecca.

Once the Holy Prophet (S.A.W.) along with his companions including Taleeb (R.A.A.) was offering prayers. Suddenly they were attacked and abused by Abu Jahl, Abu Lahab, Aqaba and others. The companions defended themselves. Taleeb (R.A.A.) attacked Abu Jahl and wounded him.

Consequently, he was over powered and he was captured by the infidels. Some people approached Hazrat Urwa Bint Abdul Muttalib (R.A.A.) and said, "See the foolishness" of your son. He was helping and supporting Muhammad (S.A.W.) so he became a victim of the infidels."

She replied, "The day Taleeb defends his uncle's sons, it will be the best day of his life because, he is the Messenger of Allah, so his defence means the defence of Truth."

(Mustadrak Hakim)

When Abdullah bin Zaid (R.A.A.) was wounded in the battle of *Uhud*, his mother, Umm Ammara (R.A.A.) treated his wounds and instead of asking him to rest, she advised, "My son ! Rise, take your sword and attack the infidels."

(Tabaqat Ibn Sa'd)

Hazrat Khansa (R.A.A.) had taken part in the battle of *Qadisia* along with her four sons. She inspired them to fight for the cause of Islam. She told them that Hereafter is a better place than this mortal world. She quoted this verse from the Holy Qur'an :

> "O ye who believe ! Endure, outdo all others in endurance, be ready, and observe your duty to Allah, in order that you may succeed." (3 : 200)

The sons were so much impressed by the teachings of their mother that they fought against the enemies and laid down their lives for the cause of Islam. *(Istiab)*

When Hajjaj had beseiged Hazrat Abdullah-bin-Zubair, (R.A.A.), about ten thousand of his companions left him and joined Hajjaj-bin-Yousuf. So much so that his two sons—Hamza and Khubaib also sought the refuge of Hajjaj. In despair Abdullah-bin-Zubair went to his mother Asma Bint Abu Bakr (R.A.A.) and related the sad tale of his helplessness. He said, "Now only a few persons are standing by me. They would not be able to face Hajjaj. If I settle with Hajjaj, I can get all I want. What is your opinion ?"

The mother replied :

> "My son ! You know yourself better. If you are sure that you are on the right path and you are inviting them towards the right, then be steadfast. Many of your

companions have lost their lives while fighting against the enemies. So do not surrender to Bani Umayya. But if you think that you have done this for the worldly cause, then you are the meanest man of the world. By doing so you have destroyed yourself and others, in vain. If you are on the right path, then it is better to die for it. The life will come to an end one day, so it is better to sacrifice it for the cause of Islam. If you try to weaken your religion, you will loose after life. Hazrat Abdullah-bin-Zubair calmly listened his brave mother and laid down his life fighting valiantly against Hajjaj-bin-Yousuf.

CHAPTER 9

WOMEN AND COLLECTIVE RESPONSIBILITIES

Islam does not lay any restriction on spiritual, social economic or political activities of women. The Holy Qur'an provides clear cut proof that a woman is completely equal to a man in terms of her rights and responsibilities.

The Qur'an says :

"Every soul will be (held) in pledge for its deeds."
(74 : 38)

It also states :

". . . So their Lord accepted their prayers, (saying) : I will not suffer to be lost the work of any of you whether male or female. You proceed one from another.
(3 : 195)

Woman according to the Qur'an is not blamed for Adam's first mistake. Both were jointly wrong in their disobedience to Allah; both repented and both were forgiven.
(2 : 35; 7 : 20-24)

In one verse (20 : 121), Hazrat Adam was specifically blamed.

In terms of religious obligations, such as the daily prayers, fasting, payment of *Zakat* (Poor-due) and pilgrimage, woman has certain advantages over man. :

The pre-Islam Arabs ill-treated the women-folk. They hated the birth of girls and buried them alive. The Qur'an forbade this practice. They gave no rights to their wives and married themselves indiscriminately any number of wives; divorcing them at their will without giving them any compensation.

The Qur'an clearly states that the marriage is sharing between the two halves of the society; its objectives, besides perpetuating human race, are emotional well-being and spiritual harmony. It bases are love and mercy. According to Islamic Law, a women cannot be forced to marry against her will. Besides all other provisions for her protection at the time of marriage, it has been specifically decreed that a woman has full right to *Mehr* or dower money.. It is not the price for a woman, as was the case in certain cultures but rather it is a gift symbolizing love and affection.

The Holy Qur'an has decreed that one should be kind to his parents. The Holy Book has specially recommened for the good treatment of mothers. The Holy Prophet (S.A.W.) has declared that "Paradise lies at the feet of mothers."

Islam granted the right of independent ownership of economic rights to the women, which was denied to them before Islam and after it (even as late as this century in some countries).

A fair investigation of the teachings of Islam will prove woman's equality with man in what we call today "Political Rights". This includes the right of election as well as the nomination to political offices.

Woman's Intellectual Capabilities

The responsibilities of woman in Islamic society are not limited. Its scope is vast and varied. Her responsibilities depend upon her mental faculties and capabilities. The Holy Prophet (S.A.W.) has said about women, "They are mentally and physically weaker." The jurists have said, "(in capabilities) man is superior to woman."

Not only that Islamic *Shariah* has accepted woman's weakness but also provided various facilities and concessions to her :

(1) She has been exempted from offering her prayers *(Salat)* during the period of menses as she remains unclean and feels weaker during that period.

(2) The period of delivery is more difficult for her. Therefore, she has been exempted from prayers during this delicate period.

(3) If her menses or pregnancy falls during the Holy month of Ramazan, she may complete her days of missed fast during some other months.

(4) She has been exempted from participating in *Jihad.*

(5) While performing Hajj, she has been allowed to leave for Mina early in the morning without passing the night of Ninth of Zil Hijja at Muzdalfa. The concession relieves her from the trouble of walking in the heavy crowd. She has been also permitted to complete her *Rami* Jumrat before reaching of other persons in Mina.

Women's Evidence

Woman is weaker than man in many aspects. Therefore, in case of woman's evidence, her reliability has been lessened. The Holy Prophet (S.A.W.) has said :

"The evidence of woman is half of the man's." ***(Bukhari)***

The law of evidence has been mentioned in five places in the Holy Qur'an. Out of which only one discusses about the evidence of woman. The Holy Qur'an says :

"O ye who believe ! When contract a debt for a fixed term, record it in writing. Let scribe record it in writing between you in (terms of) equity. No scribe should

refuse to write as Allah hath taught him, so let him write, and let him who incurreth the debt dictate, and let him observe his duty to Allah, his Lord, and diminish not naught thereof. But if he who oweth the debt is of low understanding, or weak, or unable himself to dictate in (terms of) equity. And call witness from among your men, two witnesses. And if two men be not (at hand) then a man and two women, of such as you approve as witness so that if the one erreth (owing to forgetfulness) the other will, remember. And the witnesses must not refuse when they are summoned. Be not averse to writing down (the contract) whether it be small or great, with (record of) the term thereof. That is more equitable in the sight of Allah and more sure for testimony, and the best way of avoiding doubts between you; save only in the case when it is actual merchandise which ye transfer among yourselves from hand to hand. In that case it is no sin for you if ye write it not. And have witnesses when ye sell one to another, and let no harm be done to scribe or witness. If ye do (harm to them) lo! it is a sin in you. Observe your duty to Allah. Allah is teaching you. And Allah is Knower of all things."
(2 : 282)

The law of evidence is clearly laid down in Islamic jurisprudence, specially in *'Hidayah'* and *"Durrul Mukhtar."* The law of evidence as propounded by the *Sunni* School in Islam and is explained in *Hidayah* (vol. III Page-664) is in many respects the same as the law of Moses. In the Pentateuch two witnesses at least were required to establish any charge (Num. xxxv. 30) and the witness who withheld the truth was censured a (LEV. V-1.) whilst slanderous statements and officious witnesses were discouraged (ex. xxviii. I; Lev. xix-16) and false witnesses were punished with the punishment due to the offence they sought to establish (DEUT. xix-16). According to Josephus, women and slaves were not allowed to give evidence (Ant. iv. c. 8. S. 15).

It is the duty of the witnesses to bear testimony, and it is not lawful for them to conceal it, when the party concerned demand it from them. Because it is laid down in the Qur'an (Surah 2 : 282 cited above), "Let not witnesses withheld their evidence when it is demanded from them." And again, "Conceal not your testimony for whoever conceals his testimony is an offender."

On account of woman's physical constitution, social, economic and general conditions, certain limitations have been placed on her capacity to give evidence. A woman is generally confined to her domestic chores and is rarely concerned with affairs relating to trade and commerce or matters requiring agreements and undertakings necessitating testimony.

In cases inducing corporal punishments, a woman is least expected to be a good witness. Moreover on account of her frail constitution, shyness and her inability to stand the vigour and rigour of standing in a court of law to evidence and to withstand cross examination, a woman is not a proper person.

Almost all the jurists agree that evidence of only women is enough in the matters relating to females only and of which the males are not expected to have any knowledge. Imam Shafie (R.A.) says :

> "I have not come across any scholar who has opposed the evidence of only women in the matters of birth and physical defects in the private organs of women."

Imam Zahri states :

> "It is in accordance with the *Sunnah* that as all matters relating to women are known to them only, the evidence of women is legal."

Hazrat Abdullah Bin 'Umar (R.A.A.) has also supported this view.

Hind Bint Talaq relates :

"I along with some women was at a place. There lay a

child covered with cloth. A woman, while passing there, crushed it. The mother of the child accused her of the childs' death. Ten women, including myself, gave the evidence before Hazrat Ali (R.A.A.) which he accepted."

Hazrat 'Umar Farooq (R.A.A.) did not consider the evidence, of women right in the case of marriage *(Nikah)*, divorce, *Hodood.* (Capital punishments prescribed by Allah) and murder, but it is related that four women gave their evidence before him that such and such man had divorced his wife in the state of intoxication. Hazrat 'Umar separated the wife from her husband.

Allama Ibn Hazam (R.A.), after accepting the evidence of two women equal to one man, considers the evidence of women reliable in all matters and rights. Justice Shuraih also agrees with this view. Once a case about the houshold goods was brought before him. The husband and the wife were the parties to it. The husband claimed that the goods belonged to him. But four women gave their evidence in favour of the wife and maintained that the goods belonged to the wife. The wife gave him the dower money and he gave her those goods instead, justice Shuraih accepted the evidence of the women and gave his judgement in favour of the wife.

Ayas-bin-Muavia (R.A.) has accepted the evidence of two women in respect of divorce.

It is related that Hazrat Muavia settled the dispute of a house only on the evidence of Hazrat Umm Salama (R.A.A.).

Joint Evidence of Man and Woman

There are certain matters that relate to woman and only women have their knowledge. In such cases the evidence of only women is admissible. But there are other matters for which only women's evidence is not considered reliable by certain jurists. According to them the joint evidence of man and woman is essential.

Imam Malik and Imam Shafie (R.A.) maintain that only in financial matters joint evidence is admissible. All Hanafi jurists and Usman Batti (R.A.) accept the joint evidence as the basis for the judgment in respect of all matters other than *Hudood* (Capital Punishments) and *Qisas* (Murder). Imam Sufiyan Sauri also supports this view. Even in the case of *Qisas*, the joint evidence is acceptable to him. For Tawoos (R.A.) the joint evidence of man and woman is admissible in all cases except adultery. But Ata Bin Abee Ribah (R.A.) maintains that if three men and two women give evidence in a case of an adultery, it is acceptable.

Ata-Bin-Abee Ribah (R.A.) says that Hazrat 'Umar Farooq (R.A.A.) has allowed the evidence of two women and one man in the matters of marriage *(Nikah)*. Justice Shuraih has allowed the joint evidence in the matter of slavery.

These arguments show that the joint evidence should be accepted in all matters except *Hudood* and *Qisas*. Imam Zuhri relates that Holy Prophet (S.A.W.), Hazrat Abu Bakr Siddiq (R.A.A.) and Hazrat 'Umar Farooq (R.A.A.) did not approve the evidence of women in the case of *Hudood* and *Qisas*.

Woman's Credibility in Narrating Hadis

The *Ahadis* related by women are treated as much reliable as related by men. Men and women are given equal importance in the matter of relating *Ahadis*.

Once few camels of the husband of Hazrat Abu Saeed Khudri's sister, Faria (R.A.A.) disappeared. He went in search of those camels and finally found them. But the camels attacked him suddenly, consequently he died. Faria (R.A.A.) related this matter to the Holy Prophet (S.A.W.) and said, "My husband has expired. Neither he has left food for us to eat nor any house to live in. Therefore, I want your permission to live with my brother." The Holy Prophet (S.A.W.) replied, "You should complete the period of your *Iddat* in the house where you received the information of your husband's death."

A similar case was presented to Hazrat Usman Ghani (R.A.A.) during his Caliphate. Some people told him that a similar case of Hazrat Faria (R.A.A.) was decided by the Holy Prophet (S.A.W.). Hazrat Usman Ghani (R.A.A.) summoned her. She came and related the decision of the Holy Prophet (S.A.W.). Hazrat Usman Ghani (R.A.A.) decided the case according to the decision of the Holy Prophet (S.A.W.) and ordered that woman to complete the period of her *Iddat* in the house where her husband had died.

The instance and rulings cited above would show that the majority of the Muslim Jurists and *Ulema* have decided that in all cases the testimony of women witnesses is admissible. However, according to them there may be an exception in the matters which concern the practical life of males and which are outside the sphere of a female's daily routine. In such cases the testimony of male is preferable over a female.

CHAPTER 10

WOMAN IN PRACTICAL LIFE

1. Women's Duties

Holy Prophet, Muhammad (S.A.W.) has said :

"Woman is the care-taker of all the members of her husband's family and his children. And for this she will be questioned on the Day of Judgment." *(Bukhari)*

This *Hadis* shows that woman's primary duty is to look after her home. She has been made responsible for her domestic duties. The external affairs are looked after by the husband. However, she has been allowed to leave home when any necessity arises. But Islam does not make her responsible for any duty outside her home.

As a wife she has to look after the affairs of her husband. She has to protect and safeguard the walfare and rights of the members who are under her care. She is also responsible for the protection of her husband's wealth and property. Holy Prophet (S.A.W.) has described the characteristics of a pious and faithful wife thus :

"When her husband is out of sight, she guards her chastity and wealth and property of her husband." *(Ibn Majah)*

Holy Prophet (S.A.W.) had assigned the domestic duties to Hazrat Fatimah (R.A.A.) and Hazrat Ali (R.A.A.) was to look after the matters outside the house. But this does not mean that woman has been confined to home only. Islamic

Shariah has provided full freedom to woman in respect of her rights as enjoined by the Holy Qur'an. Once Hind bint Utba (R.A.A.) complained to the Holy Prophet (S.A.W.) that her husband does not give her the money required for the domestic expenses, hence, there is no other way except that she takes his money without his knowledge. The Holy Prophet (S.A.W.) replied, "You may take money required for the maintenance of yourself and your children." *(Bukhari)*

The wife also has the right to give alms from some portion of her husband's wealth. The Holy Prophet (S.A.W.) said, "When wife spends from the wealth of her husband within the limits of *Shariah*, she gets its reward and the husband gets the reward for his earning." *(Bukhari)*

According to the Islamic *Shariah*, woman is the most suitable person for nursing and bringing up children. A companion of the Holy Prophet (S.A.W.) divorced his wife. He had a child from her, whom he wanted to keep with him. But the divorcee complained to the Holy Prophet (S.A.W.) who said :

> "Your right (of the custody of the child) is superior until you re-marry." *(Abu Dawood)*

Explaining this *hadis*, Allama Shaukani (R.A.) says : "This *hadis* proves that the mother has greater right over her child than the father, unless she re-marries." All jurists unanimously agree on this point of law. Allama Badruddin Kashani (R.A.) says :

"The right of custody *(Hizanat)* belongs to the wives because they are more loving and kind and can look after the minors more carefully and diligently." *(Badai-wal-Sanai)*

2. Women's Organization

Women are allowed to play an effective and helpful role in the Islamic society. *Shariah* allows them to form their own organization for the uplift of the society. Though such organization did not exist during the time of the Holy Prophet (S.A.W.) and *Khulafa-e-Rashideen* (Pious Caliphs) (R.A.A.) because the circumstances were different and no such need arose then. But the fact cannot be denied that women used to get together during those days also and put before the Holy Prophet (S.A.W.) the problems which they faced and the Holy Prophet (S.A.W.) listened to them. Now the circumstances are different. The Muslim women have to face various difficulties all over the world. Therefore, they can form their own organisations to solve the problems concerning women and children and they can do a lot for their upliftment.

Once a woman approached the Holy Prophet (S.A.W.) and said :

"Men are benefited by your sermons and advices, but we have no such opportunity. Therefore, we request you to givt us also some time so that we may also come to you for acquiring knowledge that you receive from Allah."

The Holy Prophet (S.A.W.) said : Well, assemble all of you on such and such day." When they all assembled at a place on the fixed day, the Holy Prophet (S.A.W.) went there and taught them the principles of Islamic *(Shariah.) (Bukhari)*

Once, the Muslim women of Madina selected a very wise woman, Asma bint Zaid, as their representative and deputed her to the Holy Prophet (S.A.W.) for the solution of their problems. She said to the Holy Prophet (S.A.W.), "I am a representative of the Muslim women. I have to say what they have to say and they have the same opinion as I have, that Allah has sent His Prophet and Messenger (S.A.W.) for men and women both. So we have faith in you and follow your teachings regarding the commands of Allah. But we, the women who observe *Purdah* (Veil), who remain confined to our homes to become the focus point of our men, who bear the children for our husbands, cannot equal the men who attend Friday congregations, funeral prayers and participate in *Jihad* and thus earn honourable status in the sight of

Allah." The Holy Prophet (S.A.W.) turned to his companions and said, "Have you ever seen a better woman who enquired about her religion so eloquently ?" The companions replied, "By Allah, we have not heard such (a good talk)." The Holy Prophet (S.A.W.) said to Asma (R.A.A.), "Asma, go and tell women whom you represent that should they obey their husbands and behave well with them, it will equalize them with the men regarding the services of men you related."

(At Targhib-wat-Tarhib)

Thus the Muslim women have represented on many occasions to the Holy Prophet (S.A.W.) for the solution of their problems. Abu Dawood relates, "When the Holy Prophet (S.A.W.) took the Oath of Allegiance from women, an elderly woman, perhaps from the clan of Muzir stood up and said, "O Messenger of Allah (S.A.W.), we are already burden on our parents and husbands and children, so have we any right to spend from their wealth ?" The Holy Prophet (S.A.W.) replied, "Yes, the things like dates which you can eat and present to others also.

The study of history shows that *Shariah* is not against the formation of separate organizations of women. The best proof is that women can form their own rows for offering their prayers in the mosques. *Sahabiyat* have offered their prayers in congregations led by women. It is related by *Refah al Hanafiya* that Hazrat Ayeshah (R.A.A.) led the obligatory prayers, *(Farz* Salat) for women and stood in their midst (i.e. she did not stand like a man in front of the rows).

(Dar Qutni)

Tamimah bint Salma relates, "Hazrat Ayeshah (R.A.A.) led the *Maghrib* prayers and stood in the middle of the women and recited the verses of the Holy Qur'an loudly."

(All Muhalla)

Hajirah bint Haseen says, Umme Salamah (R.A.A.) led the *Asr* (Afternoon) prayer and stood in our midst."

(Dar Qutni)

'Ata says that Hazrat Ayeshah (R.A.A.) used to give call *(Azan)* for the prayers and say *Iqamat* (call for preparing rows for prayer) also. And she used to lead the prayers and stand in the middle of the women.

Hazrat Ayeshah relates that she used to lead the optional Night prayers *(Taraveeh)* during the month of *Ramazan* and stand in the middle of the row.

(Kitab al Asaar-Imam Abu Yousuf)

Khairah relates that Hazrat Umm Salamah (R.A.A.) used to lead their (Women's) prayers during the month of *Ramazan* and stand in the middle of the row. *(Muhalla-Vol. II)*

In fact, *Salat* (Prayers) is a sort of mini-organization of the *Ummah*, therefore, the leading of prayers is called the *Imamate-Sughra.* When the Holy Prophet (S.A.W.) passed away from this world, the question of his successor arose. The *Muhajireen* (Immigrants) proposed the name of Hazrat Abu Bakr Siddiq (R.A.A.) and to support his suitability they cited that Holy Prophet (S.A.W.) had selected him to lead the prayers during his lifetime. On the basis of this *(Hadis)* it can be rightly said that women can form their own organization within the framework of the Islamic *Shariah* for the purpose of solving their own problems. And they can be allowed by law to perform various duties of the society for the welfare of the mankind.

3. Woman and the Leadership

It is a fact that Islam does not permit a woman to lead the Muslim Nation *(Ummah)* because she does not possess the qualities of leadership, and it shall be against her nature to entrust a woman with the task for which she is not capable. This kind of step will lead the *Ummah* to nothing else but destruction. The Holy Prophet (S.A.W.) has said :

"Men were destroyed when they obeyed women."

(Bukhari)

"A nation which has entrusted its leadership to a woman cannot be successful." *(Mustadrak Hakim)*

Imam Shaukani, explaining this *Hadis*, says, "This is a fact that woman is not capable of patronising and ruling. And it is not proper for any nation to assign leadership to a woman, because it is necessary to abstain from the act which is harmful." *(Nail-al-Autar)*

The consensus of the *Ummah* against the leadership of woman is not based on hatred or contempt. But the Islamic *Shariah* doest not want to burden her with such heavy and onerous responsibilities, considering her weak physique and delicate temperament. The scholars and the jurists maintain that the leader *(Imam)* of the Muslims must be well versed in Islamic law and intelectually far sighted and thoughtful. He must be able to take right and prompt decision at the crucial times like war and peace and have firm determination to enforce it otherwise he will surely fail to lead the Muslim *Ummah*. These qualities are found only in men and lack in women. Therefore, they cannot be assigned heavy responsibilities which are beyond their capacity.

4. Suitable Responsibilities for Women

Though women cannot be assigned the leadership of the *Ummah*, she can be made responsible for certain social services which she can render according to her capabilities. Allama Ibn Ilham Hanafi (R.A.) says :

"The *Shariah* says that her intellect is faulty but every body knows that it is not so to the extent that she may not hold any responsibility. You should know that she can be the manager and trustee of trust and the guardian of the orphans."

Likewise, there are many other responsibilities that can be assigned to a woman for the welfare of the Muslim society and uplift of women and children. The main consideration should be that she must be able to perform the duties assigned to her. She has to abide by certain rules and principles of *Shariah* while taking up any task in the social set-up.

CHAPTER 11

GUIDING PRINCIPLES FOR WOMEN

1. Realization of Correct Position

Woman has to realize her real position in the Islamic society which aims to establish the environment free from all evils. She is the architect of the domestic life. Therefore neither the state should assign her such duties which are injurious to herself, nor she has the right to destroy the domestic life and take part in such activities which may prove harmful to herself, her house and the society. She is not supposed to solve the political problems but look after the affairs which are solely meant for her.

2. Obedience to Husband

Islam is the complete code of life and provides guidelines for every aspect of human behaviour. Its main object is to relieve man from slavery of man and establish the sovereignty of Allah over the entire mankind. It leads to peace and tranquility. For this reason man has been assigned superiority over woman in certain respects.

The Holy Qur'an says :

"Men are in charge of women, because Allah has made the one of them to excel the other, and because they spend their property (for the support of women)."

(4 : 34)

Therefore, the husband can restrict his wife to such principles which are necessary for the well being of the conjugal life, and the wife has to obey her husband in all cases except which oppose the principles of Islam. The Holy Prophet (S.A.W.) has said that for a believer, after fear of Allah, a virtuous wife is the best endowment of Allah. About one of the good qualities of a virtuous wife, the Holy Prophet (S.A.W.) said, "If he (husband) orders, she will obey."

(Ibn Majah)

Once somebody asked the Holy Prophet (S.A.W.) to explain the good qualities of a virtuous wife. The Holy Prophet (S.A.W.) replied :

> "One who pleases her husband when he sees her, and obeys when he orders. And she must not oppose him by an act which he does not like." *(Nasai)*

Hazrat Abdullah bin 'Umar (R.A.A.) relates that the Holy Prophet (S.A.W.) has said :

> "There are two types of persons whose prayers *(Salat)* do not go beyond their heads (that is, not acceptable to Allah); the one is the slave who runs away and returns and the other is a wife who disobeys her husband and approaches not to him for forgiveness and promises not to disobey him in future." *(Tabarani)*

In order to clarify the legal position of husband and wife, the Holy Prophet (S.A.W.) said on the occasion of the *Hajjat-ul-Wida.*

> "Treat your wives nicely because they are under your custody." *(Trimizi)*

The wife is under the control of her husband and, therefore, she has to obey him. On another occasion the Holy Prophet (S.A.W.) said about wife.

> "The wife, who believes in Allah and the Day of Judgment, is not allowed to admit any man whom her

husband does not like. She must not got out under the circumstances which he does not approve. And she must not obey anybody else in respect of the affairs of her husband nor she must quarrel or fight with him when he comes." *(Mustadrak Hakim)*

Though wife is allowed to offer her prayers in the mosque but it is better for her to get the permission of her husband. In this respect Hazrat Abdullah bin 'Umar relates the advice of the Holy Prophet (S.A.W.) to a husband :

"If your wife asks for permission to go to the mosque to offer her prayers, she should not be stopped (without a valid reason)." *(Muslim)*

Hence, it is crystal clear that the wife should take the permission of her husband to leave the house not only for offering prayers in the mosque but for any other purpose, as well.

In the light of these *Ahadis* it is a proven fact that the wife cannot leave her house without permission of her husband. The Islamic *Shariah* allows the wife to leave her home for any good cause but not without the permission of her husband. This has been done to keep off evil and maintain harmony in the conjugal life.

But there are certain exceptions to this rule, that is, wife is allowed to leave her home without the permission of her husband under certain unavoidable circumstances which are pointed out by the Hanafi jurists thus :

"The wife is not allowed to leave her home without the permission of her husband except in certain restricted circumstances. The circumstances are : She can leave the house if it is going to collapse; if she has a juristic problem which her husband cannot solve, she can leave the house and proceed to the juristic school for its solution; If she has to go for *Hajj* and there is *Mahram* (A close relative with whom her marriage is forbidden) to accompany her; the husband can allow her to go and that will be no sin for him. Similary she is not bound to take permission of her husband for visiting her parents or near relatives." *(Fatawa Qazi Khan)*

This juristic argument proves that wife is bound by certain principles to obey her husband and it allowed, certain special concessions only under unavoidable circumstances. The husband also can impose certain restriction on her activities in the house.

Allama Ibn Nujaim says :

"The husband has the right to prevent his wife from earning her livelihood because this is the duty of her husband. Similarly the husband can restrict her from performing any other virtuous work which is not obligatory." *(Al Bahr-al-Raiq-Vol. IV)*

The husband has this right because he himself is responsible for the maintenance of his wife and children. However, if the husband is unable to provide the necessities of life for her children, the wife is permitted to look for and earn money for the maintenance of the family. Besides, as Allama Ibn Abedin (R.A.) says, "There are certain expenses of the wife for which the husband is not bound, hence, the wife can work at home and earn money to meet such expenses. "He has further said the husband can prevent her from doing such extra hard work which affects her health. It is the right of husband to keep his wife hail and hearty and beautiful."

Allama Ibn Abedin further says :

"A husband can prevent his wife from all such activities which either deprive him of his rights or cause harm, or for which she has to leave her house. But here is no reason to prevent her from any activity which causes no harm to him." *(Al Durral Mukhtar)*

The Islamic *Shariah* imposes restrictions on the movement of the woman in her own interest as well as for the welfare of the whole family. And every good family contributes and helps in the establishment of a good society. Ultimately good societies make a good and disciplined nation.

Islam considers the home as heaven for her faith and morals, whereas there is always a fear of losing them, outside the home. Holy Prophet Muhammad (S.A.W.) has said;

> "Women is to be kept in privacy, therefore, keep her confined in the house." *(Tirmizi)*

Speaking psychologically, Islam wants the conjugal ties to be strong and everlasting, because this relation is very delicate and may be shattered even by a slight misunderstanding. A good husband would never like his wife to go out very often because this creates many problems. Allama Ibn Ilham has said :

> "Wife's going out of home very often opens the door for evil, specially when she is young and the husband may be well-bred and courteous, is a gentleman. *(Fath-ul-Qadeer)*

3. Restrictions on Free Mixing

A Muslim lady is allowed by *Shariah* to leave her home with the permission of her husband to perform her religious, educational and social services, but she should keep in mind the fact that she has been restricted from mingling with the male strangers. Islam confines her to home because her presence amongst the men who are strangers gives rise to moral degeneration. If a woman breaks the law of *Shariah* and enters any field, with however good intentions, her step will be considered against the principles of Islam because it leads to troubles and destruction.

No one, on earth, can be more God-fearing than the Holy Prophet (S.A.W.) and no one else can be compared with him (S.A.W.) so far as the loftiness of character is concerned. Hence, the fact remains that some women of his (S.A.W.)

time who came to him to take pledge, to serve the cause of Islam, were not allowed to clasp his (S.A.W.) hand, although the men took the Oath of Allegiance by placing their hands on his (S.A.W.) hand, Hazrat Ayeshah (R.A.A.) says :

"The Holy Prophet (S.A.W.) took the Oath of Allegiance from women orally according to this Quranic verse. "O Prophet ! If believing women come unto thee that they will ascribe nothing as partner unto Allah, and will neither steal nor commit adultery nor kill their children, nor produce any lie that they have devised between their hands and feet, nor disobey thee in what is right, then accept their allegiance and ask Allah to forgive them. Lo! Allah is Forgiving, Merciful." (60 : 12)

"His (S.A.W.) hand never touched the hand of any women while taking the Oath of Allegiance, except the hand of his (S.A.W.) wife." *(Bukhari)*

On another occasion she has said ;

"No, by Allah ! (The hand of the Holy Prophet (S.A.W.) never touched the hand of any other woman. He (S.A.W.) took woman's Oath of Allegiance orally. Then he (S.A.W.) used to say, "Go, I have taken your Oath of Allegiance orally." *(Muslim)*

Sometimes some women tried to place their hands on his (S.A.W.) hand while taking the Oath of Allegiance, but the Holy Prophet (S.A.W.) said, "I do not shake hand with women, my addressing a group of hundred women is as good as addressing a single woman. Therefore, there is no need to take separate Oath of Allegiance from each woman." *(Nasai)*

As it has been said before, Islam aims to establish a society free from all evils and provides peaceful living for the whole mankind. Therefore, it is absolutely essential to keep the men and women separate in all matters whether educational, cultural, martial, social or political. Thus according to Islamic *Shariah* women are not allowed to mingle with other men. As a matter of fact it is not possible to have healthy environment in any society if the intermingling of men and women are allowed. Hence prevention is better than cure.

In Islamic society neither co-education nor co-cultural programmes are allowed. A Muslim woman is not permitted to take military training along with other men. Nor she can participate in games or recreation with men. Whether it is a market place or an assembly hall, Islam considers intermingling of the two sexes at any place, as undesirable.

Women attended the sermons of the Holy Prophet (S.A.W.) but separate seating arrangments were made for them. They never sat alongwith the men. Islam is the *Deen* for all times. Hence even in the modern times women can participate freely in all activities and functions, within the limits of the *Shariah* provided separate arrangments are made for them. Hazrat Abdullah Ibn Abbas (R.A.A.) describes the *Eid* prayers in these words :

> "First he (the Holy Prophet (S.A.W.) led the *(Eid)* prayers and delivered the sermon *(Khutba)*. Then alongwith Hazrat Bilal (R.A.A.) he came towards the women and addressed them." ***(Bukhari)***

Interpreting this *Hadis* Hafiz Ibn Hajar says, "Hazrat Ibn Abbas says that the expression 'the Holy Prophet (S.A.W.) came towards the women' makes it distinctly clear that the women were separate from the men and not intermingled with them." ***(Fath-ul-Bari)***

According to another narration, the Holy Prophet (S.A.W.) first led the prayers and then delivered the sermon. Afterwards he felt that the women could not hear him properly, so he came (a bit closer) to them and advised them. ***(Bukhari)***

This *Hadis* clearly shows that the women were quite at a distance and therefore, they could not hear the Holy Prophet (S.A.W.) properly.

Though no regular military training was given to women during the time of the Holy Prophet (S.A.W.), yet they were always found ready and fit for tendering their services during emergencies. But now the Islamic states can train women for active participation in modern walfare. However, the condition of the Islamic *Shariah* shall ever remain in force. There shall be altogether separate arrangements for their training and participation in wars.

4. Woman in War

War is a big obstacle in the way of human life. It stops progress and brings devastation. In such situation the entire nation is involved and the circumstances take such turn that it becomes impossible to apply the normal laws and principles. The rules that are framed for normal conditions, do not remain effective in an emergency.

The war creates such dangerous and dreadful situation that the set rules become ineffective and every individual has to become active and helpful for the cause of Islam and Muslims. So the participation of women in war also becomes inevitable. This does not mean that the law 'women should not mingle with men' is broken but automatically suspended to some extent for the time being during the emergency.

The Holy Prophet (S.A.W.) and his companions had to face very critical situation during wars. In the first place they had not yet attained the political stability in the country and in the second place they were numerically less and had not enough equipment to fight.

On the other hand, the enemies were in large number and well equipped. They also brought a large number of women with them who encouraged the men to fight and also provided medical aid to the sick and the injured. But the Muslim women remained attached to the domestic duties only, therefore they knew nothing about war. Ultimately the participation of Muslim women in war became inevitable.

Hazrat Ayeshah (R.A.A.) says, "I was with the Holy Prophet (S.A.W.) during a battle. I was very thin and lean in those days. The Holy Prophet (S.A.W.) asked his companions to go ahead. After that he (S.A.W.) told me to have a race. I won in the race and the Holy Prophet (S.A.W.) just kept quiet.

After a long time, when I had already forgotten all about this event and became fat, I accompanied the Holy Prophet (S.A.W.) on a journey. This time also the Holy Prophet (S.A.W.) asked the companions to go ahead and called me to have a race. But this time the Holy Prophet (S.A.W.) won the race and replied smilingly "It is my victory this time." *(Durrul Sameen)*

However, the Holy Prophet (S.A.W.) directed the Muslims that women's participation in battles must be restricted to absolute necessity only. Hence the history of Islam shows that women scarcely took part in the important battles. Besides, it was essential for every woman, wishing to take part in the battle, to take prior permission of the Holy Prophet (S.A.W.).

This restriction was to eliminate the fears and doubts from the minds of the Muslims. After taking all factors into consideration, the Holy Prophet (S.A.W.) allowed women to join the battle. He (S.A.W.) always took care while allowing a woman that she was essentially required for the battle and that the necessary arrangements were made for her safety. The Holy Prophet (S.A.W.) never allowed any woman to participate in the battle unless he (S.A.W.) was fully satisfied in this regard.

Once some women for the sake of *Jihad* joined the army without permission. When the Holy Prophet (S.A.W.) came to know about this, he warned them. Hashraj bin Ziyad relates from his grandmother :

> "I accompanied the Holy Prophet (S.A.W.) for the battle of *Khaiber*. There were five other women also. When the Holy Prophet (S.A.W.) came to know about

this fact, he (S.A.W.) summoned us through a man. When we went to him we found him angry. Then angrily he asked us, "With whom have you come and with whose permission have you come ?" *(Abu Dawood)*

This shows that firstly the women were required to have permission of the Holy Prophet (S.A.W.) for participation in the war and secondly they were to come with their clan or with very reliable persons. The Holy Prophet (S.A.W.) was angry with the grandmother of Hashraj bin Ziyad (R.A.A.) and other women because they evaded these pre-conditions.

Umm Sinan Aslamiya (R.A.A.) relates :

"When the Holy Prophet (S.A.W.) decided to move towards *Khaiber*, I went to him and said, "I intend to join you in this battle. There, if necessary, I shall sew the leather bags and treat the sick and the injured (May Allah forbid). I shall look after the belongings of the soldiers." The Holy Prophet (S.A.W.) said, "May Allah grant His bounties, you may join us. Some other women of your and other tribes had sought my permission which I have already granted. All these women shall be your companions. You may join your own clan or if you wish you can join us." I said, "I shall accompany you." He replied, "Well, then join my wife Umm Salama (R.A.A.)." So I joined her. *(Tabaqat Ibn Sa'd)*

The study of the Islamic history shows that the ladies accompanied generally their real relations, father, brothers or sons on the war fronts.

The fact cannot be denied that Islamic states may have to face such situation in every age. So the women, within the limits of the *Shariah* and above mentioned conditions, can serve the cause of Islam and their country directly or indirectly. Islam is the practical *Deen* and will remain ever dynamic. Its laws are for the entire mankind and for all times. It controls the activities of men and women for the welfare of the entire mankind. Its target is always to uproot the evil.

5. Women in the History of Islam

Woman has achieved an important and significant place in the history of Islam. But the West has done a great disservice to the history by distorting and mis-interpreting the facts of the Islamic history.

The freedom that West has given to woman is not the freedom in real sense of the term. In fact, it is a licence and an attempt at exploitation of woman for the satisfaction of man's sensual desires only. This kind of freedom has made the Western society corrupt and evil.

The Western culture teaches woman to rebel against her own home and encourages her to become a plaything for the men in the so-called modern society. Whereas, Islam has given her the freedom of equal rights, honour and dignity. The main place of her activities is her home. Besides, she is allowed to leave her home when the necessity arises. The freedom of women by West brings disgrace to her, whereas the freedom granted by Islam elevates her status and she becomes an honourable member of the society.

The West has painted a very wrong picture of a historical event. After the martyrdom of Hazrat Usman Ghani (R.A.A.), the administration of the state was greatly disturbed. When it became difficult to bring to book the assassins of Hazrat Usman Ghani (R.A.A.), Hazrat Ayeshah (R.A.A.) entered the arena of politics and endeavoured to enforce the laws of *Shariah* on the culprits. Her struggle for the cause of Islam brought her to the stage of leadership which is the right of man alone. It was an emergency and there was no man to lead the Muslim nation and fight the forces opposing Islam. The situation was so grave that she declared war even against Hazrat Ali (R.A.A.) who tried to confront her.

The West has interpreted this event wrongly and derived very mischievous conclusions from it. The Western historians base their arguments on this particular event of the Islamic history and maintain that Islam has granted equal rights in the field of politics, that is, a woman can become the leader of the nation. Hence, her participation in politics and social activities cannot be prohibited according to *Shariah*. They say that men and women can intermingle freely in every sphere of human life. But this notion is absolutely false and baseless. It is a fabrication to defame Islam.

It is a fact that Hazrat Ayeshah played a leading role on account of unavoidable circumstances. That was an exception and does not make a rule. The rule remains the same that woman cannot be assigned the leadership of the Muslim *Ummah*. Women was never allowed to play this role during the time of the Holy Prophet (S.A.W.) and *Khulfa-i-Rashideen* (R.A.A.).

The teachings of Islam restrict the activities of woman to her home and allow her to leave it only in inevitable circumstances. The leadership of the nation was never assigned to woman nor she ever claimed it. Though the Holy Prophet (S.A.W.) and *Khulfa-i-Rashideen* (R.A.A.) faced great difficulties and hurdles, yet woman was never entrusted with any responsibility for their solution.

During the long period of Islamic rule, a number of battles were fought but woman was never made the commander-in-Chief of the Muslim army. Woman was never appointed as a Governor by the Holy Prophet (S.A.W.) or by any of his four Caliphs. She was not assigned any responsible post in the department of finance or the judiciary. After the demise of the Holy Prophet (S.A.W.) the Muslims never elected any woman as their Caliph.

America is the most advanced and prosperous country of the world. If one or two persons are found there poor, it would not make America a poor country. Similarly if Hazrat Ayeshah (R.A.A.) played a leading role in the politics of her time, it would not mean that Islam allows the leadership of woman. The act of an individual cannot become the rule of the *Shariah*.

If an individual act of Hazrat Ayeshah (R.A.A.) can serve as a model for the Muslim *Ummah* then why not the act of other *Ummahatul Momineen* and venerable *Sahabiyat?* If Hazrat Ayeshah's (R.A.A.) battle against Hazrat Ali (R.A.A.) can serve as a precedent, then why not the action of Hazrat Umm Salamah (R.A.A.)? Because, when Hazrat Ali (R.A.A.) left for Basrah to fight against Hazrat Ayeshah (R.A.A.), Hazrat Zubair (R.A.A.) and Hazrat Talha (R.A.A.), Hazrat Umm Salamah said to him :

"*Ameerul Momineen* : If we accompany you on this occasion, it will amount to disobedience to Allah and you would not approve this act of ours. We would have come with you if these two factors were not there. My cousin (brother) is here. I love him more than my life. He will go with you and take part in the battle."

(Tarikh Kamil)

On the other hand she wrote to Hazrat Ayeshah (R.A.A.):

"Your position is like a door between the Holy Prophet (S.A.W.) and the Muslim *Ummah*. And your modesty is the veil of honour. But you have unveiled yourself. Remember, the Holy Qur'an has laid certain restrictions on you, so do not step beyond the limits. Allah wants you to be at home, hence do not leave it and do not come to the battlefield. Allah is at the back of the Muslim *Ummah*. You know how much Holy Prophet (S.A.A.) loved you ! Had he wanted to assign such responsibilities, he would have assigned during his life-times, but he did not. And you know that if the pillar of Islam falls,the women cannot re-erect it and if it cracks, the women cannot repair it. Were the women fit for *Jihad*, the Holy Prophet (S.A.W.) would have allowed you. The *Jihad* of women is that they should keep their eyes down and protect themselves.

Had the Holy Prophet (S.A.W.) seen you on the back of a camel wandering about the mountains and monds, what would have been your explanation ? One day you will have to present yourself before the Holy Prophet (S.A.W.) and you have disregarded the principle of veil and ignored the law of Allah ?

Had I done what you have done, I would have felt ashamed to enter the Heaven. Therefore, I request you to observe *Purdah* (veil) established by the Holy Prophet (S.A.W.) and make your home your castle. You can be real well-wisher of the *Ummah*, if you remain at home instead of coming to the battlefield. If I tell you a *Hadis* of the Holy Prophet (S.A.W.) you would certainly pounce upon me like a snake to bite me." *(Al-Iqdul-Farid)*

This kind of criticism came not only from Hazrat Umm Salamah (R.A.A.) but from many other respectable personalities of the *Ummah.*

When Hazrat Ayeshah (R.A.A.) reached Basrah on her mission, she wrote to Zaid bin Sauban addressing him as son, "Immediately join the mission which has been launched to avenge the blood of Hazrat Usman (R.A.A.). And if you do not want to joint, at least keep your people away from favouring Hazrat Ali (R.A.A.),," After reading this letter, Zaid bin Sauban said, "May Allah have mercy upon *Ummul Momineen.* We were commanded to launch *Jihad* and she had to be at home. She has ignored the restrictions imposed upon her and she wants me to obey. She has taken over the responsibilities assigned to us and she is preventing us from carrying out our duty. Then he replied to Hazrat Ayeshah (R.A.A.) "Indeed I am like your real son and you are my mother. Unless you give up your struggle and return home I shall be the first person to leave." *(Tabari)*

Another well known personality of Basrah and companion of the Holy Prophet (S.A.W.), Jariah-bin-Qudama says to Hazrat Ayeshah (R.A.A.), "The martyrdom of Hazrat Usman Ghani is lighter than your action. Allah has bestowed upon you the honour and commanded to observe *Purdah* (Veil) but you have ignored it. One who considers war against you rightful, can consider taking of your life also rightful. Just imagine in what delicate position you have put the people. Therefore, if you have come of your own free will, then go back to home and if you have been compelled then gain the favour of the people against him and you reach home.

Hazrat Abu Bakr (R.A.A.) a well known companion of the Holy Prophet (S.A.W.) says, "I would have joined Hazrat Ayeshah (R.A.A.) in the battle of Jamal. But the saying of the Holy Prophet (S.A.W.) saved me. When he (S.A.W.) received the news of the coronation of the daughter of Kasra, he (S.A.W.) said, "The nation who hands over its reigns to a woman, cannot be successful." *(Bukhari)*

An eminent companion like Hazrat Abdullah bin 'Umar (R.A.A.) says, "For Hazrat Ayeshah (R.A.A.) her home is better. The criticism of these respectable contemporary personalities was not just to oppose Hazrat Ayeshah (R.A.A.) out of grudge or enmity but to remind her of the commandments and the limitation of Allah imposed upon woman. Even Hazrat Ayeshah (R.A.A.) had great respect for them who criticised her for participating in the battle instead of remaining at home. Therefore, the main issue was not the criticism but the strict observance of the principles of Islam.

The history of Islam shows that the Muslims had to face numerous difficulties in the early period. But the men themselves were able to solve the problems of the *Ummah* and never invited the women to participate in their struggle in person. Hazrat Ayeshah (R.A.A.) herself survived for about fifty years after the demise of the Holy Prophet (S.A.W.) and saw ups and downs in the lives of the Muslims and remained aloof. She took no active part to improve the prevalent unfavourable conditions. This proves that she considered the home, the real place of her activities.

Hazrat Ayeshah (R.A.A.) adhered to the principles of Islam during her whole life. Hence a single incident cannot become the means of denial for the facts of the whole life. The wise thing is to study the circumstances, that led her to the battlefield.

The facts of history prove that dissatisfaction prevailed among the common people against Hazrat Usman Ghani (R.A.A.) during the last years of his Caliphate. The people had started criticism against him. The situation became so grave that notorious elements attacked Madina and consequently Hazrat Usman Ghani (R.A.A.) was martyred. Though the elders of the Muslims strived to avert the catastrophe but failed. And the *Millat* (nation) had to suffer a tremendous loss. It was the first and the peculiar event that shook the whole *Ummah.* The wise men thought that it was their defeat and the victory of the ruffians, and if immediate action was not taken against them, then Islam would become a plaything in the hands of the wicked. Some of them decided to punish according to *Shariah* all those who participated in the martyrdom of Hazrat Usman Ghani (R.A.A.), otherwise the *Ummah* would lose the honour, and power would slip into the hands of the enemies of Islam. Such mischief-mongers would select a caliph and kill him when they so desired, and there would be no power to check them. The senior members of the community like Hazrat Zubair (R.A.A.) and Hazrat Talha (R.A.A.) held this view. Maleh bin Aaf-ul-Salma asked Hazrat Zubair (R.A.A.). He replied :

"What do you want?" "We are preparing the people to avenge the blood of Hazrat Usman Ghani (R.A.A.) so that it may not go waste. If we allow it to go unavenged then the supreme authority among us would become weak. If they are not corrected and made to respect the authority, then they would continue killing the caliphs at will. By Allah, it is absolutely necessary to avenge the blood of Hazrat Usman Ghani (R.A.A.). You do not realize the consequences that would follow." *(Tarikhur Rusul)*

There was yet another group which considered the unity of the *Ummah* as the most important issue. It observed that dissension and anarchy was spreading fast. As the whole *Ummah* had taken the form of a rebellious army; as such they considered unwise to raise the question of avenging the blood of Hazrat Usman Ghani (R.A.A.) as it would create, further trouble. They, therefore, decided to consolidate the

Ummah hence with this end in view they elected Hazrat Ali (R.A.A.) as their caliph. The majority of the inhabitants of Madina supported this group. Consequently the supporters of the other group left Madina and moved to some other cities. Some of them reached Mecca where *Ummahatul-Momineen* lived. The latter had no knowledge of developments in Madina, because they had left Madina long before and had come to Mecca with the intention of performing *Hajj.* When they enquired from the people coming from Madina about the prevalent conditions in that city, they gave a quite different account of the situation there. According to them, the riffraffs and unruly persons had taken over the city of Madina and have installed there as caliph.

Hazrat Ayeshah (R.A.A.) enquired from a relative, "What is the situation ?" He replied, "The lawlessness prevaling in Madina has hit hard the people there." Hazrat Ayeshah (R.A.A.) felt sorry and put another question, "Let me know whether the situation is in our favour or against us ?" He replied, "I do not know all this; but the people were left without any caliph for eight days after the martyrdom of Hazrat Usman Ghani (R.A.A.). After that the Madinities and the ruffians who had overpowered the city gathered around Hazrat Ali (R.A.A.)." *(Tabari)*

Another relative of Hazrat Ayeshah (R.A.A.) informed her that "Hazrat Usman Ghani (R.A.A.) has been martyred and the people have agreed to take the Oath of Allegiance in favour of Hazrat Ali but the real power is in the hands of the rogues." *(Tabari)*

Hazrat Zubair (R.A.A.) and Hazrat Talha (R.A.A.) had reached Mecca. They did not like to take the Oath of Allegiance in favour of Hazrat Ali (R.A.A.). Naturally their feelings were different from other people. When Hazrat Ayeshah (R.A.A.) asked them about the situation in Madina they replied :

"We have left Madina because we were in minority and afraid of the rebels and bedouins. When we left Madina, the people were in a state of confusion, unable to distinguish between right and wrong; so much so that they had no courage even to defend themselves." *(Tarikhur Rusul)*

Hazrat Zubair (R.A.A.) and Hazrat Talha (R.A.A.) and their supporters now started paving the way for the improvement of the conditions. They invited the Muslims to avenge the death of Hazrat Usman Ghani (R.A.A.). For this purpose they needed the support and sympathy of *Ummahatul Momineen* who were fortunately available there. They were also very much affected by the developments in Madina and their support could put life in any movement that could be launched. Hazrat Zubair and Hazrat Talha (R.A.A.) therefore, approached *Ummahatul Momineen*, specially, Hazrat Ayeshah (R.A.A.) and Hazrat Hafsah (R.A.A.) who had great influence over the society and requested them to support their struggle for the re-establishment of Islamic principles. But all of them excepting Hazrat Ayeshah (R.A.A.) considered it beyond their capacity and refused to lend their support. As such Hazrat Ayeshah alone, returned to Madina.

Probably Hazrat Ayeshah (R.A.A.) thought that if the courage and determination of Hazrat Aboo Bakr (R.A.A.) could crush the scourge of heresy, this *Ummah* still could crush the rebellion it faced then, they needed only the guidance and inspiration. Hence she decided to join the movement launched for reformation of the people. With this end in view she reached Basrah. The Governor of Basrah,. Usman bin Hanif sent Imran-bin-Haseen to ascertain her intentions. Hazrat Ayeshah (R.A.A.) replied :

"The mischief-mongers and defectors from tribes have waged war in the sacred city of the Holy Prophet (S.A.W.); they have been instrumental in spreading heretical innovations and have joined hands with renegades and innovators, and have invited the wrath of Allah and his Prophet (S.A.W.) upon themselves. Moreover they have slaughtered the Caliph of the Muslims without any justification. Thus they have shed blood of an innocent *Imam* and robbed the money and property of the people over which they had no right.

They have polluted the sacred city of Madina and violated the sanctity of the Holy month. I have come out to show the people what the miscreants have done and what is the state of the people left there after we left the place, and how they can be reformed and corrected." Then she recited this verse of the Holy Quran :

> "There is no good in much of their secret conferences save (in) him who enjoineth almsgiving and kindness and peace-making among the people. Whoso doeth that, seeking the good pleasure of Allah, We shall bestow on him a vast reward.
> (4 : 114)

And she said, "Our position is that we are ordering you to do good and abstain from what is evil."

(Tabari, Al Kamil, Ibnul Asir)

Qaqa asked, *Ummul Momineen*! What brings you here?" She replied, "O my son, I have come here to reform the people."

(Al-Kamil)

Her statement proves that neither she had any ambition for power nor had she come to wage war against Hazrat Ali (R.A.A.). She aimed at reforming the *Ummah* through her good offices. Imam Ibne Taimiya (R.A.A.) says :

"Hazrat Ayeshah (R.A.A.) neither waged war nor she had come with that intention. She had come just to correct the people. She was under the impression that she had to leave home (at that critical time) for the good of the Muslims."

(Minhajul Sunnah, page 295)

No doubt, she had to fight against Hazrat Ali (R.A.A.) but this was against her intentions and wishes. She was compelled by the circumstances to fight a battle against him.

This is a fact that Hazrat Ayeshah (R.A.A.) was the leading personality amongst the *Ummah*. The people considered her their leader and guide. All matters of the community were settled with her consultation and approval. But it cannot be proved by any instance from history that she ever claimed the leadership of the *Ummah* for hereself. She always thought that she was just a guide and the well-wisher of the Muslims.

The people were always ready to sacrifice everything at her instance but they never elected her as their legal caliph. When the difference of opinion arose amongst the people as to who should lead the prayers, Hazrat Zubair (R.A.A.) or Hazrat Talha (R.A.A.), the matter was decided with the consultation of Hazrat Ayeshah (R.A.A.) and ultimately Hazrat Abdullah bin Zubair was appointed to lead the prayers. But the name of Hazrat Ayeshah (R.A.A.) was never suggested for this purpose by any one. This was the attitude of the people, who supported Hazrat Ayeshah (R.A.A.) and according to them her position was higher than those of Hazrat Talha, Hazrat Zubair and Hazrat Abdullah bin Zubair (R.A.A.).

It is a self-evident fact that Hazrat Ayeshah (R.A.A.) had to take such steps owing to an extreme emergency, which she would have never taken in normal circumstances. It was an exceptional event which occurred owing to unavoidable circumstances and it can never become the rule for all times.

CHAPTER 12

SEXUAL RELATIONS

In Ancient Time

Sexual relation is the only means to maintain the continuity of the human race. Hence the superstitious man of ancient time considered the sexual instinct as a supernatural power. It was the basis for his life and death. The people of Egypt, Sudan, West Africa, Europe and Asia felt helpless before this so-called supernatural power. It was necessary for them to please this power and avoid its wrath for the continuation of their generation. The people of certain races had carved such statutes which were the clear manifestation of sexual relation. The people of a certain race in India made the phallic-worship as a part of their religion. Even now they carve idols resembling sexual organs and worship them in their temples.

The ancient man was ignorant hence superstitious. He considered the process of generation as supernatural and a part of his religion, because he thought that children were necessary for the maintenance of life and defence against hostile forces. This process brought the family into existence. The families grew into tribes and tribes into a nation and state.

In ancient time, the relation of sex differed from clan to clan. Some clans practised monogamy and some other polygamy. But the various systems were not the result of social and economical necessities. They came into existence owing to the arising situation. However, there were certain customs which were based purely on the satisfaction of sexual desire. The fact cannot be denied that sexual urge is extraordinarily strong and irresistible. Hence it is wrong to think that the people in ancient ages had any consideration for the interest of the society in relation to the satisfaction of their sexual instinct. On the contrary, history proves that sexual urge had almost overpowered the social welfare and the society had to suffer. The lives of innumerable people were destroyed and the people lost their peace of mind due to it. It created law and order situation and human life became miserable Intrigues, quarrels, and murders have always been the common feature of the human rapacity for sex.

Life of Abstinence

The complexity of sex gave birth to the idea of altogether avoiding sex. Some people thought that the suppression of the sexual urge would provide relief and peace to the mankind. According to them sex was a disturbing factor of life and it was not possible to have peace and happiness unless they got rid of it. This gained popularity in Egypt, Greece, India, China and Europe. It tried to keep away man from sexual functions and created a sort of hatred for it. They considered the salvation of mankind therein.

It is a historical fact that after Jesus Christ, the Christianity also adopted this view. The custom of celibacy was introduced and even today the Catholic priests are not allowed to marry. They observe celibacy and keep themselves away from sexual desire. It is said that when the famous Monk Sevius became very old and weak, his friends and disciples advised him to abandon his abode in the forest and dwell in some urban area. He agreed to their request on the condition that he would like to live in a town place where there were no women. As it was impossible to find such a place, he remained in the same jungle until his death.

It is said that St. Basle had vowed not to see the face of woman unless under dire necessity. St. John did not see the face of any woman for forty eight years. At last his wife sent word to him that should he not come to see her, she would commit suicide. He replied that he would come to her at nights, consequently, his wife saw him in her dream.

The hatred for sex reached such a stage that those celibates tried to escape from their mothers and sisters also. Once a celibate was travelling with his mother. On the way he came across a stream over which there was no bridge. Hurriedly, he tried to wrap his whole body with a piece of cloth. The mother was surprised and asked him the reason. He replied that as he had to carry her on his shoulder while crossing the stream he would not like to touch her body at all because that would destroy his all good deeds.

St. John had a sister who loved him very much. When he became a monk and left home he did not see his sister for many years. The sister wished to see him so she wrote many letters to him but he always refused. At last she herself decided to see him in the forest. The saint did not like the idea and wrote to her that he would come to see her. Though he came to see her but in disguise and went away. The sister complained to him for not keeping his promise. He replied that he had come to see her but by the grace of Jesus she could not recognise him. He also wrote that she should not wish to see him any more.

It is said about St. Payman that he suddenly left home alongwith his six brothers and went to the jungle. Imagine the plight of the mother whose all seven sons left her alone. When it became unbearable for her, she also went to the forest. When she reached there, they were leaving their cottage. On seeing her, they got embarrassed and turned back. The mother at once followed them but before she could reach them, they shut the door from inside. She stood there helplessly and cried bitterly. Hearing this, St. Payman came close to the door and asked her the reason for crying. She replied sobbingly, "Your separation has made me so sorrowful. Don't you know that I am your mother? Have I not suckled you? Have I not brought you up? Is it the reward for my services? Have you forgotten all my rights?" But this entreaty had no effect on him. He replied that she would be able to see them after her death. The poor mother helplessly returned home.

There is a similar story about St. Samuel. He had also left his home. When twenty seven years passed and his mother came to know of his whereabouts, she went to the jungle to see him personally. She also implored, and cried in vain, but the son did not allow her to see him. When he saw his mother very much in distress, he said that he would come to see her very soon. She waited for him for three days but he did not turn up. At last his mother died of the shock.
(The Moral History of Europe, Part-II)

Thus it is seen that hatred towards woman led to another unnatural way of life. Monking created a lot of problems. Adultery became common and illegitimate children were born in the Christian society. The Christianity, instead of reforming the people, became the source of evil practices and moral corruption. It is but logical that any step which is against the Law of Nature would bring disaster and chaos in the human society. The sexual urge is natural, hence it cannot be suppressed without evil consequences.

Islam has made marriage compulsory for this reason. In March, 1957 the British Neurologists examined the background of eleven thousand Patients of mental sickness and came to conclusion that the patients had reached that stage owing to non-marriage. The doctors advised that if a man wants mental peace and wants to escape from mental disease, he must marry.

The seventeen member countries of U.N.O. including Pakistan made research and found that the average age of married men was more than the bachelors and widowers. If the average age of all men of these countries is calculated, the average age of married men comes approximately to fifty seven years and those of unmarried men amount to thirty years; and the highest average age is of the married women.

Abstinence from sexual relation not only affects the individual but it destroys his social relations also, and ultimately it degenerates the whole society. Therefore, celibacy is against Nature; and whatever is against Nature should be eschewed. Woman is not the source of evil but the centre of attraction and means of continuity of human race. It is the Law of Nature which cannot be challenged by man.

Extremism

Since the ancient times there existed another view which was just the opposite of the practice of celibacy. According to this view, sexual relation was considered natural, but there were no set principles for its satisfaction. The group of people who held this view went to another extreme and considered nothing lawful or unlawful for the satisfaction of sexual desire.

If celibacy was escapism from the evil of sensualism, extremism was the defeat of human courage and determination. It opened the door to adultery and prostitution. The society could not remain safe and sound.

The history shows that sexual lawlessness was very common during the ancient times. Once a woman was brought before Jesus Christ by some men. They made her stand in the middle and said, "O Master, this woman has been caught red-handed while commiting adultery. What is your order against her?" Jesus Christ replied, "The one who is innocent amongst you, should stone her first." Hearing this, they left one by one and only Jesus Christ remained there because he was the only innocent person there. *(The Bible)*

Sex in Pre-Islamic Arabia

Hazrat Ayeshah (R.A.A.) describes the state of Arabia before the advent of Islam. "There were four systems of satisfying the sexual urge, prevalent in Arabia. The first system was the regular marriage. According to this system, when a man wanted to marry a girl, he would send the message to her parents. If the proposal was accepted, the marriage was solemnized after the payment of the dower.

The second method was that if a man wanted a child of a prominent or well-known man, he would send his wife to him who would remain with him until she became pregnant.

The third system allowed a maximum number of nine men to marry one woman. If a child was born, she attributed its birth to any one of them and it was called his child.

According to the fourth system, prostitution was legalized. The prostitutes hoisted flags at their doors and any man could satisfy his sexual desire there. And the children born to such women were recognized by the expert physionomists and handed over to the man responsible for their birth. And such man had to accept them without any objection." *(Bukhari, Abu Dawood)*

Sex in India

There were eight prevalent methods in India for the satisfaction of sexual desire. "These methods were classified as eight kinds of marriages . . . . . .

1. *Brahm Vivah* : The marriage by mutual consent of a boy and a girl who have been observing strict abstinence and are religious, good-natured, of spotless character and learned.

2. *Dev Vivah* ; Giving away of an embellished daughter to a son-in-law while performing *yagya.*

3. *Arsh Vivah* : Giving away of a daughter in marriage after realizing some return from the son-in-law.

4. *Prajapat Vivah* : The marriage for the purposes of promoting the cause of religion.

5. *Asur Vivah* : The marriage in which both the bride and bride-groom get something.

6. *Gandharv Vivah* : The marriage in which the bride and bridegroom have come to the terms somehow.

7. *Rakshas Vivah* : Carrying away of some one's daughter by force for the purpose of marriage.

8. *Pishach Vivah* : The marriage by raping a mad, intoxicated or sleeping girl. *(Satyarth Prakash).*

Besides, there were other forms of ancient customs. According to a custom known as "*Niyog*" among Brahmins, a childless wife was allowed to have children at will by the younger brother of her husband or any other relative with the permission of the father-in-law or some other authority."

(Manu Smrity)

And all these eight methods were considered right and lawful. The barren women passed nights with the Hindu priests in order to get conceived. This practice was very common and considered lawful in the Hindu society.

CHAPTER 13

SEX IN THE MODERN AGE

Western Trend

The Western idea about sexual relation has been very very strange and astonishing in every respect. It holds that man is also an animal and so can satisfy his sexual desire like other animals. It lays no restriction or limitation on sexual indulgence and enjoyment, and encourages its unbridled freedom. The Westerners think that the sexual thirst should be quenched without any moral consideration and should not be buried under the debris of morality. As if, their sole aim of life is nothing but sexual pleasure.

According to the Westerners, it is narrow mindedness of the religion to consider adultery and fornication immoral and unlawful. As an animal is not questioned as to how it satisfies its sexual desire, similarly a human being should not be questioned. But they forget that what they think and practice is not only immoral and unlawful but also unnatural. This trend demoralises the people, wpreads evil and the whole society becomes corrupt and lewd.

According to them only such act which is harmful to others should be discouraged and stopped forthwith. Thus, this philosophy has made them beast of the worst type. Consequently a flood of sexual extravaganza is let loose, free intermingling of men and women is encouraged, pornographic literature, nude pictures and blue films flood the market, and liquor and intoxicating drugs have submerged the entire Western Society.

Glimpses of Sexual Chaos

A London student vividly describes the sensual atmosphere in a magazine thus : "When he gets up early in the morning and goes to wash his face in the basin near a window, he sees a huge crowd of women down on the road. When he is ready to go to college after having his breakfast, a maid servant appears for cleaning work. In some houses,an old maid servant is found and in some other houses very young and often corrupt ones. It is a time for office. There is a big queue for tickets. He is also waiting in the queue. There is a woman in front of him, there is a woman behind him. Frequently their bodies come in contact with each other. When he enters the lift full of men and women, it is impossible there for him to save his body from touching that of the women in front of him. Even his eyes cannot escape the sight of woman. In order to avoid gazing the woman opposite him, he looks up at the lift. There are large and attractive commercial advertisements. In all these advertisements, women is the focal point of attraction. Some advertisements are of those companies which manufacture underwears. Hence the woman is depicted in these advertisements. In some other advertisements the woman is displayed just putting off her underwear. Thus the evil of nudity with all its charms is daringly exhibited in these advertisements. Hence, he removes his eyes from those advertisements and starts gazing once more at the woman facing him.

Same is the situation in a railway train. It is full and overcrowded. He is caught in the crowd which consists of more women. Helplessly, he has to lean against a woman.

When he reached his college, he found a seat vacant in the class and occupied it. The whole class room was full within a short time. A young girl comes and takes her seat next to him. Her body freely rubs him and some times her legs also. *(Asia, Weekly, Lahore, dated 18.3.1957)*

Sometime back a woman was produced before a court in Italy on the charge that she roams on the roads only in her underwears. The learned Judge evicted her on the ground that the nude body of a beautiful woman does not harm any one.

Once the editor of "New York Times" visited Japan and gave his personal impressions in an article entitled Worlds Nude City—Tokyo. He says :

"I happened to visit the house of a Japanese journalist. I was disturbed very much by the situation that I had to face. I pressed the bell and waited at the door. The door opened and I saw a nude woman with wet hair. She told me that the journalist was not there and that she was his wife; the woman was bathing and came out to tell me without any hesitation."

The editor relates another incident in the same article :

"I had an opportunity to attend a dinner party. Generally a Japanese hosts a dinner party in some posh hotel, but this gentleman invited me to his house. After the dinner the programme of dancing and singing started which was also arranged by him. A guest over-drank and lost his control. He got up and started dancing with a young girl. While dancing he removed her clothes one by one and made her stark naked. Seeing this the host and the guests burst into laughter."

This kind of nudity and free intermingling of men and women has become very common even in temples. It is said that in a village of South Rhodesia a unique custom has been adopted in a church to induce attendance. It is called "Production of Brotherhood". The men hug and kiss the women and make love with them before prayers. Consequently the number of attendance has increased to such an extent that the management of the church had to build more rooms to accommodate the people.

According to the report submitted by a Commission appointed by the Government of U.S.A., the main cause of sexual crimes like rape, kidnapping, murder for sex, venereal diseases and pugnacity are the films, produced in Holywood. If these films are not censored strictly, a time will come when whole of America will be filled with rogues, murderers, adulterers and dacoits. These films have made the dacoits, heroes of the young generation. The youths have adopted the dresses of the docoits as a fashion. Kidnapping and rape are considered the sign of masculine valour and bravery. Many girls run away from schools and colleges without informing their parents. The Commission was distressed to observe the fact that once the character of America was a model to follow for the whole world, but now it has reached the height of degeneration.

Pornography has become so common that even the law is unable to curb it for the reformation of the society. In July, 1957 the Supreme Court of America has given the Judgement that the Constitution does not permit pornography at all. Criticising this judgement a pornographic writer wrote that in pornography-loving America, law cannot stop pornography. It has become popular because the people of America like it. Hence any law against it, would be a mockery. The Americans are facing various problems and are most afraid of the topic of sex, but they also seek satisfaction from it. It is wrong to conclude that punishment can put an end to nudity and pornography.

In France, a committee was appointed to investigate the alcoholic drinking. According to its report, 23% men and 43% of women use water for drinking, and contrary to this, 82% of men and 60% of women drink liquor. There are also some men and women who drink mixture of wine and water. Their ratio is 4% and 9% respectively. The committee has submitted that the deaths by over-drinking have increased twelve times within the period of last ten years.

It is said that in West Germany, an owner of a drinking house flows a stream of beer on his birthday every year and allows every man and woman above eighteen years of age, to drink it freely. In 1960 25,000 persons drank from it.

The President of International Board of Alcohol Prevention, Dr. Robert Pears, has written that 50 to 75% sexual crimes which take place, are owing to intemperance. In 1955 the Medical Board of France had declared that no chaste woman can be found in France and French are proud of it. A Judge, Marshal Scott has written in his book entitled, "Prostitution" that in Paris eight thousand prostitutes come out from house and hotels in the evening and start their business. About two thousand such women throng the streets in the afternoon searching for customers. About fifty thousand customers meet these ten thousand prostitutes every night."

Writing about 1956, the British Police Commissioner said that this year the rape cases were the highest since the Second World War. And the number of such crimes was more than three times this year than 1938. On 4th September, 1957 a Committee, comprising lawyers, doctors, priests and three women, under the chairmanship of Sir John was appointed to report on the prevailing immoral conditions in Britain. The committee published its report after three years, according to which prostitution was considered inevitable as it served the demand of a group of people. Money is no doubt an incentive for prostitution; but it is definite that the girls and women join this profession deliberately.

According to the report published by the British Medical Association 1959, in Britain, every third woman has confessed that she had already sexual relations before her marriage and that every twentieth child is illegitimate.

Commenting on moral degeneration, a medical specialist, Mrs. Hudson says :

"Our walls of culture are about to collapse. Their bases have become weak and the pillars are shaking. Who knows when the whole building would give way. We are observing for the last so many years that people are not ready to adhere to discipline and rules. The only way to keep it alive is to restrict the free mixing of men and women. The peple of this society have focussed all their attention on the satisfaction of their sexual desires. Hence all their constructive energy is being wasted. There are other irregularities also. For instance, the attraction of men and women towards their own sex. This waste of human energy has reached its critical stage."

An idea of moral degeneration in the West can be had from the following quotation.

"Let it be enough to say that immorality between near relatives, even sometimes between father and daughter and between brother and sister are not very uncommon in certain popular quarters of our great towns."

(Towards Moral Bankruptcy, by Paul Bureau P. 35)

Paul Bureau further says "The life portrayed by the French stage gives an impression that married couples in France are by and large deceitful to each other and disloyal matrimonially."

(Ibid, P. 43)

This author quotes Emile Pouresy, who reports several instances of indecensies which he collected from various theatres :

> "At B (the name of the theatre) monologues and songs are grossly obscene; the tableaux and dramatic scenes go so far as to picture the sexual relations. At N the little songs, the most obscene monologues, and some gestures which are veritable public outrages on chastity, are applauded by children and young people under the approving eyes of their parents." *(Ibid p. 18)*

Dr. Edith Hooker in her book, "Laws of Sex" says that even in cultured societies it is not uncommon to find girls, seven years old or so, involved in clandestine love affairs with boys of their own age group with whom sometimes they have sex relations also. She relates the case of a seven-year old daughter of a respectable family who had her first sex-experience with her own elder brother and some of his friends.

(Laws of Sex p. 328).

Judge Ben Lindsey, writes in his book. 'The Revolt of Modern Youth' on pp. 81-82. "Sex overwhelms them (American Children) before their minds and their powers of restraint and judgment are mature enough to cope with it."

A Baltimore physician reports that within a year or so, more than a thousand cases of fornication with girls under 12 were prosecuted in Baltimore city. *(Laws of Sex p. 177)*

The rising number of divorces, increase in sexual crimes and the excessive use of sex in radio, television, advertisements and other departments are the prelude to the destruction of Americans. Our environment is full of nudity and semi-nudity. So much so that the commercial advertisements are replete with sensualism. It appears that sensuality has become the part and parcel of the American life.

(American Sexual Revolution, by Prof. Peter M.S.)

Effects of Sensuality

Sensuality is dangerous in every sense and destroys man in many ways :

Firstly; it destroys human health. Nature has provided this vital energy in human being which if misused and squandered, will cause irreparable damage to the entire organism of human system.

Secondly; it causes impotency in the person and renders him unfit from procreation. The man limits his activity to sexual satisfaction and never thinks of having a family life in the society. Thus he becomes a preventive element in the way of human generation.

Thirdly; the sex-haunted women are killing their offsprings in the name of birth control and abortion is no more a crime for them. The government provides physicians' help in practising birth control. According to a report of Associated Press of America, more than two hundred thousand illegitimate children are born there every year. An American institution known as U.NC. grants allowance to an unmarried mother of ten children for her nine children only, out of 10

Fourthly; the persons who aim at only sexual satisfaction, become malicious and anti-social. They destroy peace and tranquillity.

Fifthly; sensuality turns humanity into irrational animality. The animal instinct makes man and woman immoral and creates a continuous source of misery and suffering.

It is a fact that uncontrolled indulgence in sensuality and lewdness not only harms human health but destroys peace and tranquility of the society. The present Western culture based on free and unbridled sex, instead of enabling the Western people to live a happy life, has landed them in social chaos and anarchy. It has failed to solve any problems of the people or provide them with proper guidance. It has not been able to meet the challenge of the time. As against this, Islam has not only led the world in the fields of culture and civilisation, it has provided its followers with a compact and all embracing system covering the minutest details of the various departments of human life.

CHAPTER 14

SEXUAL RELATIONS IN ISLAM

Balancing Power

Islam is the only *Deen* (way of life) that has succeeded in solving the sexual problems and maintaining the moral value of desire and relieves from its slavery which destroys human character altogether. Islam is not only a religion for the performance of certain rites, but it is "*Deen*" or the code of life formulated by Allah. It has provided the perfect guidelines for the sexual relations between man and woman.

Negation of Celibacy

Islam negates celibacy which is unnatural and ruins human life. It does not permit escaping from the problems of conjugal life, for achieving pleasure of Allah Conjugal relation is natural hence a necessity of life.

The Quran syas :

"We sent many prophets before you and also bestowed upon them wives and children." (13 : 38)

The Holy Prophet (S.A.W.) has said :

"*Nikah* (the marriage contract) has been the *Sunnah* of the Prophet." *(Tirmizi)*

Celibacy is unnatural and wrong because it is a man made formula and has no sanction from the Creator. The Holy Quran has made it explicitly clear :

"It is they who have themselves adopted seclusion and monastic way of life, although We had ordained the obedience of Allah and not celibacy upon them. But they disregarded even their own-invented religion, as they ought to have done." (57 : 27)

The Holy Prophet (S.A.W.) has said :

"There is no escape from *Nikah* in Islam."

(Musnad Ahmad)

Hazrat Ayeshah (R.A.A.) relates, "The Holy Prophet (S.A.W.) has forbidden the practice of castration."

Hazrat Samurah (R.A.A.) relates, "The Holy Prophet (S.A.W.) has prohibited abstinence from marriage and the world."

(Tirmizi—Nasai)

Hazrat Sa'd (R.A.A.) relates "The Holy Prophet (S.A.W.) forbade Usman bin-Maz'oon (R.A.A.) from, getting himself castrated. Had he (S.A.W.) allowed Hazrat Usman to do so, we would have followed suit."

(Bukhari, Muslim, Tirmizi, Nasai, and Ibn Majah)

Imam Nawavi (R.A.) has remarked on the basis of this *Hadis* "Castration of man, whether infant or adult, is forbidden by Allah."

Hazrat Anas (R.A.A.) says, "The Holy Prophet (S.A.W.) directed us to marry and prevented us from celibacy."

(Sunan Darimi)

Sa'd bin Hisham thought of observing celibacy and consulted Hazrat Ayeshah (R.A.A.), who replied, "Have you not heard the words of Allah that We have sent many Messengers before and bestowed upon them wives and children also." "This proves that celibacy is not the way of the true followers of prophets. Therefore, shun the idea of celibacy."

(Nasai)

Hazrat Ibn Abbas (R.A.A.) asked Sayeed-bin-Jubair, "Are you married?" Sayeed replied, "No." Hazrat Ibn Abbas (R.A.A.) said, "Then marry; celibacy is not the sign of piety because the highest man, the Holy Prophet (S.A.W.) had the highest number of wives." *(Bukhari)*

Hazrat Anas (R.A.A.) has related that three men enquired from one of the wives of the Holy Prophet (S.A.W.) about his (S.A.W.) prayers. When she told them about his (R.A.A.) prayers, the men found it very short. They thought, "A shorter prayer is enough for him (S.A.W.) because he is a sinless person. But we are sinners top to bottom, therefore, we must pray more and more." As such one of them said, "Henceforth, I shall pray the whole night and would never sleep." The second one said, "I shall fast continuously without break." The third one said, "All troubles are caused by marriage, hence, I shall never marry and pass the rest of my life in praying Allah." When the Holy Prophet (S.A.W.) learnt about this, he (S.A.W.) said :

"By Allah, I am the most pious and most God-fearing man among you, but I keep *Nafl* (optional) fasts and also discontinue them; I pray at night and also sleep. I also marry women and this is my way of life. Hence, he who shuns my way (Sunnah), he is not from me." *(Bukhari)*

Hazrat Ayeshah (R.A.A.) has related the Holy Prophet (S.A.W.) as having said, "*Nikah* (marriage) is my *Sunnah* and the person, who does not follow my *Sunnah*, has nothing to do with me." *(Ibn Majah)*

These *Ahadis* prove that there is no place for celibacy in Islam. And one who wants to remain celibate for the sake of piety, he is utterly ignorant of the teachings and the practice of the Holy Prophet (S.A.W.). The fear of Allah compels a man for prayers as well as for marriage.

The Holy Prophet (S.A.W.) has said :

"Whatever you spend for the pleasure of Allah, you will be rewarded for that, you will get reward even for that

morsel which you put in the mouth of your wife."
(Bukhari—Muslim)

The Holy Prophet (S.A.W.) further said :

"The *Deenar* (Gold-coin) which you have spent in the way of Allah, to free a slave, to help the poor, on your wife and children, only that *Deenar* would fetch the highest reward which you spent on your wife and children." *(Muslim)*

Considering the wife and children obstacle in the way of love for Allah, Sa'd-bin-Hisham divorced his wife and wanted to sell out all his land and give the money for the cause of *Jehad*. Some people of his clan came to know of his plan. They came to Hazrat Sa'd (R.A.A.) and informed him that six men holding similar views had approached the Holy Prophet (S.A.W.) but he (S.A.W.) forbade them from doing so and said :

"Is my life not a good example for you to follow?"

The Holy Prophet (S.A.W.) never neglected his conjugal duty and fulfilled his responsibilities throughout his life. It is his *Sunnah*. Hence, whosoever destroys this right, follows not the *Sunnah* of the Holy Prophet (S.A.W.), he has strayed away from the right path and shun the *Sunnah* of Hazrat Muhammad (S.A.W.).

Usman-bin-Maz'oon (R.A.A.) had given up his interest in his family-members and devoted his days and nights to prayers. The Holy Prophet (S.A.W.) came to know of this fact, and summoned him. When he came, the Holy Prophet (S.A.W.) said to him, "Usman, I have not been commanded to practise asceticism. Tell me, have you given up my *Sunnah?*" Usman-bin-Maz'oon (R.A.A.) replied, "O Messenger of Allah (S.A.W.) ! No, I am the follower of your *Sunnah.*" The Holy Prophet (S.A.W.) said :

"My *Sunnah* (practice) is this, that I pray at night and also sleep. Sometimes I keep fast and sometimes I do not. I follow the principles of marriage and divorce. This is my way of life. Whosoever goes astray from my way of life, he is not from me. Usman, fear Allah. As you have your duty to Allah, you also have your duty to your wife and children. Your guests have rights over you and you have right over yourself. Hence, make efforts to fulfil all these obligations." *(Musnad Ahmad)*

The Holy Prophet (S.A.W.) received similar information about Abdullah bin 'Amr bin Aas. (R.A.A.) and said similar words to him, "Do not get yourself lost in prayers so much that you forget your duties towards your wife, children, guests and yourself." *(Bukhari)*

Once Hazrat Salman Farsi (R.A.A.) went to see Hazrat Abu Darda and found his wife in Shabby dress and asked, "Is everything alright with you?" She replied, "Your brother Abu Darda has nothing to do with the world. He is always busy with his prayers and has no time for me." In the meanwhile Abu Darda came and offered meal to Hazrat Salman Farsi (R.A.A.) and said that he would not be able to join him because he is fasting and begged his pardon. Hazrat Salman Farsi (R.A.A.) said that he would not eat unless he eats. At last, Abu Darda (R.A.A.) broke his fast and ate with him. At night he began his preparations for prayers. Hazrat Salman said that it was the time for rest, hence he should sleep. After sometimes Abu Darda again woke up for the prayers. Hazrat Salman said "Not yet." At the end of the night Hazrat Salman himself woke him up and they offered their prayers together. After that Hazrat Salman Farsi (R.A.A.) said to Hazrat Abu Darda (R.A.A.) "Allah has His rights over you and also your wife and children have rights on you. So try to fulfil all the rights. The fulfilment of one duty should not cause the negligence of other duties." When the Holy Prophet (S.A.W.) was informed about it, he (S.A.W.) approved Hazrat Salman Farsi's (views) and said that he (Hazrat Salman R.A.A.) was right. *(Bukhari)*

It can be rightly concluded that one who does not fulfil his duty towards Allah is a sinner. Similarly one who neglects the duties towards his wife and children is also a sinner. He will be accountable to Allah on the Day of Judgment.

Normal Sexual Functions

Islam permits the satisfying of sexual desire only in accordance with the injunctions of the Holy Quran. The principles of sexual relation are clearly stated by Allah in His book. Besides, we have the practice of the Holy Prophet (S.A.W.) He said :

"To have sex with wife is also a *Sadaqa* (charity)." *(Muslim)*

Allama Ibn Ilham Hanfi (R.A.) has written in the light of the Holy Quran and the *Sunnah*, "It is better to perform the conjugal rights than to shun it and get engrossed only in prayers." *(Fath-ul-Qadeer)*

Islam is against all such ideas which teach to keep off from women. Naturally man is attracted toward woman. Hence, he cannot keep off from her unless he adopts some unnatural means. The people of Hazrat Lut (Lot A.S.) were inclined towards the person of their own sex. Prophet Lut (A.S.) condemed his nation and directed them to follow the natural course, that is, to have sexual relations with women only.

The Holy Quran says :

"O My people ! Here are my daughters; they are purer for you." (11 : 77)

Man is generally defeated by his emotions. Most of the people adopt unnatural means in the absence of the law. A very few people have control over their emotions. But a Muslim cannot go astray because there are rules for his guidance. If he follows not, he commits sins for which he will be punished. Islam has laid down the principle of marriage according to which every person must marry according to Islamic *Shariah* for the satisfaction of sexual desire. The only natural and lawful means of satisfying sexual desire is *Nikah* (legal marriage). Emphasising the importance of *Nikah*, the Holy Prophet (S.A.W.) says :

"Whosoever has means and capability for marriage, but does not marry, is not from me." *(Bukhari)*

A man named Abu Azdeyad was leading the life of celibacy. Hazrat 'Umar (R.A.A.) said to him that either you are impotent or indulging in evil practices. Referring to these words, the famous scholar Tawoos (R.A.) said to another such man who avoided marriage, that either he should marry else he (Tawoos) would say the same words, to him what Hazrat 'Umar (R.A.A.) has said to Abu Azdeyad.

(Ahkamul Quran)

The Holy Quran says :

"Any one of you who is not in a position to marry a free woman of a decent family, then he should marry a Muslim slave girl (after, freeing her)." (4 : 25)

Undoubtedly, sometimes, man faces such circumstances that he is unable to fulfil his conjugal responsibilities. The Shariah has emphasised to keep in such circumstances as many fasts as possible, so that he may not go astray. Hazrat Abdullah bin Mas'ood relates the saying of the Holy Prophet (S.A.W.) :

"O youth ! If a person amongst you is capable to marry, he must marry, because it keeps his eyes down and protects him from evil. But, whosoever is unable to do so, he should resort to fasting because the fasting would shield him (against the evil.)" *(Bukhari)*

Maliki and Hanafi jurists are unanimous that when a man is unable to check his passions even after fasting, and he is also unable to afford a maid, then he must marry, provided he is sure that he would commit adultery if he did not marry.

However, they differ in their opinions regarding the maintenance and payment of the dower for marriage.

The Hanafi and some Maliki jurists maintain that a man must be in a position to provide maintenance to his wife at the time of marriage, otherwise he would resort to unlawful means. Thus he will have to run into another vice in order to avoid the first one. But the majority of the Maliki opine that it is unnecessary to emphasize the condition of maintenance on the question of marriage. If he is sure that he would commit adultery, he must abide by the *Shariah* in order to avoid that evil. In their opinion, even if there is a fear of committting adultery, he must marry. The Hanbali jurists are more strict in this respect. They maintain that even if there is a doubt for committing adultery, the man must marry. It is immaterial whether he is in a position to provide maintenance or not. However, he must endeavour to earn livelihood lawfully for his family.

Imam Ibne Taimiya (R.A.A.) says :

"If a man desires to marry and fears that he might commit obligatory duty of *Hajj.* And if there is no fear of adultery, he should prefer *Hajj.* Imam Ahmad has based his elucidation on the narration of pious and reliable people. If the devotion is of the nature of collective obligation for instance, education and *Jihad* and if there is no fear of adultery then the preference shall be given to such devotional duties. If the situation is contrary to this, the *Nikah* shall be preferred."

(Akhtiyarat, Shaikhul Islam Ibn Tammiya).

Adultery is Forbidden

As the Holy Quran is the complete code of life, it provides guidance and principles for the satisfaction of the sexual desire also. These principles are the commandments of Allah, hence they are quite natural and scientific. All unnatural ways and means, including adultery, are forbidden in Islam. The Holy Quran says :

"Nor come nigh to adultery : For it is a shameful (deed) and an evil, opening the road (to other evils)." (17 : 32)

The Holy Quran also explains the characteristics of the Believers :

"Those who avoid heinous crimes and shameful deeds, and when they are angry, even then forgive." (42 : 37)

In Islam adultery is a great sin, therefore, the believers should always keep off and never go near it under any circumstances. They possess spotless character as the Holy Quran says :

"Those who invoke not, with Allah, any other god, nor slay such life as Allah has made sacred, except for just cause, nor commit fornication; and any one who does this (not only) meets punishment." (25 : 68)

Explaining further the good qualities of the Believers the Holy Quran says :

"And those who guard their chastity, except with their wives and the slave-girls whom their right hands possess for (this) they are not to be blamed. But those who trespass beyond this, are transgressors." (70 : 29-31)

The *Shariah* has permitted only two ways for satisfaction of the sexual desire; the one is to marry and the other is to have slave-girls. The way other than these two are not allowed at all." *(Muqaddama Ibn Rushd)*

Allama Ibn Qayyim says :
It is unlawful to have sexual relation with any woman. Hence its legality should be sought in *Shariah* only and any allowance from outside it, would be unlawful."

(Zad-ul-Mua'rii)

The philosophy behind the guided-sexual relation is to encourage virtues and prevent vices in the human society. The doctrine of Islam is natural and scientific, hence it allows what is right and lawful and forbids what is wrong and unlawful. Lawfulness leads to prosperity and unlawfulness makes human life miserable. Explaining the solemnity of *Nikah* and evil consequences of adultery, the Holy Quran says :

> "Allah doth wish to make clear to you and to show you the ordinance of those before you, and (He doth wish) turn to you (in mercy) and Allah is All-knowing, All-wise. Allah doth wish to turn to you, but the wish of those who follow their lusts is that ye should turn away (from Him) far, far away. Allah doth wish to lighten your (difficulties) : for man was created weak (in flesh).
> (4 : 26-28)

Islam condemns and prohibits adultery because it is dangerously destructive for human society. It is animality and suits to animals only and not to mankind. It is explicitly laid down in the Holy Quran :

> "We have sent down to you revelations making things clear, and illustrations from (the story) of people who passed away before you, and an admonition for those who fear (Allah). Allah is light of the heavens and the earth. The parable of His lights is like a niched lamp. The Lamp is enclosed in a glass. The glass is very shining like a brilliant star. The Lamp is lighted from a blessed tree, an olive neither of the East or the West, whose oil is pure and luminous as if it would glow itself though no fire may touch it. Light upon Light. Allah doth guide whom He will to His Light. Allah doth sent forth parable for man and Allah doth know all things."
> (24 : 34-35)

The chosen people of Allah always followed the commandments of Allah in respect of the satisfaction of the sexual desire and avoided all other unlawful ways. They were always blessed by Allah because they led the mankind on the right path and saved from sexual chaos and anarchy. Their teachings were the warning against unlawful practices which always brought misery and were hindrance to the success of human life.

The nation which indulged in sexual vices never survived and perished forever. The sex-mania deprives man of his wisdom and sensibility.

The Islamic law of sexual relation relieves man from the slavery of sex and makes him righteous and God-fearing. It shows the path of happiness and prosperity.

Allah has not banned the sexual relation but laid restrictions on the unlawful ways for its satisfaction. Man is weak and susceptible to sexual pleasure. He cannot suppress his sexual urge and as such suppression is also not desired in Islam. It allows neither celibacy nor debauchery.

Islam wants man to be pious, virtuous and God-fearing. Human nature likes and appreciates good qualities because they provide mental peace and tranquillity. Therefore, Islam prohibits all unnatural and unlawful sexual relations. In fact virtuous life is the path that leads to secure Hereafter. Therefore, the true guidance is the 'Light of Allah'.

Training of an Individual

No collective movement can be successful unless an individual working for it, makes himself suitable for it. Every society endeavours to mould the life of an individual accorrding to the principles set by it. Islam gives prime importance to the reformation of an individual in the society. In this respect, Islam is always optimistic. It treats with respect every person of the world and strives to show the right path to the straying ones.

The training of Islam is not for a particular aspect of life but for all aspects of life. Its teachings relieve man from the slavery of man, in fact, from all evils of the world, and leads him to the right path of happiness in the world as well as that of Hereafter.

The Concept of Nobility

In Islam adultery is an evil, and evil cannot be reconciled with human nature. Only virtues and piety appeal to him. Because his greatness lies in being good and virtuous and not vicious. If a man is enticed by an evil, his act is unnatural and confined to his ownself. Such exceptions are always found in human society, and exceptions do not form the part of a rule. The law of Nature is that human being inclines to goodness and abhors vices. The best example of this dictum is that a man feels aversion when he does something wrong. The fact cannot be denied that even a wrong doer knows that he is doing wrong. And wrong is wrong, it cannot become right under any circumstances.

The history of the world is replete with numerous examples that only the men of high character have become eminent in the world and they are always loved by the people. But the fame of the Muslim is not limited to this world only. His next-world is also secured. The Holy Quran and the *Sunnah* of the Holy Prophet (S.A.W.) are the only guidance for the real happiness of mankind here as well as in the Hereafter.

There is no room for evil in Islam. Whereas the adultery is a shameful act and against the law of Allah, hence it is to be avoided at all costs. The Holy Quran made it crystal clear thus :

> "And when they do some lewdness they say : We found our fathers doing it and Allah hath enjoined it on us, say : Allah, verily, enjoineth not lewdness. Tell ye concerning Allah that which ye know not. (7 : 28)

The Voice of Conscience

Man, by nature, likes goodness, therefore his inmost thought rejects vices. He has been endowed with intuitive qualities which repels all external pressure leading to evil doing.

Man's conscience plays a very important role in guiding him in all aspects of life, specially in warding off evil. This world is full of many charms which are unlawful in Islam.

When a Muslim is attracted towards such a thing, his conscience pricks him and reminds him that however attractive a thing may be, if it is unlawful, it must be avoided at all costs, because that is the commandment of Allah. His duty is to please Allah and not his unlawful desires. Hence, he has to keep his linen clean from all vices. The voice of conscience always outweighs the evil. However, if continuous pressure is used against it, this effect is lost gradually. Islam makes conscience more sensitive and powerful to counter the evil forces of the world which destroy human values. Nawwas bin Sam'aan relates that the Holy Prophet (S.A.W.) said :

> "Virtue is good moral character and sin is that which pricks your conscience and you may not like that others should know it." *(Tirmizi)*

Therefore, a good man never likes to involve himself in evil practices. And when his conscience is clear, he feels happy and lives with dignity and honour. The Holy Prophet (S.A.W.) said :

> "When your good deeds please you and when your vices become unbearable for you, then know that you are a *Momin* (True believer)." *(Mishkat)*

The Incentive to Virtuous Action

Islam stimulates a person for good deeds. In fact, all the prophets of Allah have taught the same thing, that is avoidance of evil, because evil leads to shamelessness. Once a person becomes shameless, he or she can do anything. Therefore, the Holy Prophet (S.A.W.) said :

> "The parts of the teachings of the previous prophets which have reached the people include that when a person becomes shameless he can do anything."
> *(Bukhari - Abu Dawood)*

Why morality has been a part of the teachings of all the prophets ? The reason was explained by the Holy Prophet

(S.A.W.) himself. Once Hazrat Sa'd (R.A.A.) asked the Holy Prophet (S.A.W.) that if a man sees another man committing adultery with his wife, would his conscience permit him to go and find four witnesses according to the Holy Quran ? If such a case, may Allah forbid, happens with him, he would kill the man. When the Holy Prophet (S.A.W.) heard him, he (S.A.W.) addressed the gathering and said :

"Are you surprised to hear what Sa'd (R.A.A.) has said? By Allah, I am more self-respecting than him and Allah is more self-respecting than me. And for this reason He has forbidden all kinds of shameful acts whether apparent or hidden." *(Bukhari, Muslim)*

This shows that the evil like adultery is intolerable in Islam. It is against all norms of life. Hence it is to be condemned. The teachings of Islam are such that make a man morally sound and strong. His attitude remains normal and fascinating. The Holy Prophet (S.A.W.) is the best pattern of human perfection. It is said about him.

"The Holy Prophet (S.A.W.) was more bashful than a virgin in veil. Whenever any incident relating to shamelessness took place, he (S.A.W.) did not like to relate it and his (S.A.W.) dislikeness for it appeared on his (S.A.W.) face and we could observe it." *(Muslim)*

The Holy Prophet (S.A.W.) was the perfect man and he (S.A.W.) has taught mankind the lesson of virtue and piety and advised to keep off from evil.

Bahz bin Hakeem relates from his grand father. I inquired from the Holy Prophet (S.A.W.), "O Messenger of Allah (S.A.W.) ! How far should we hide our body and how far not ?" The Holy Prophet (S.A.W.) replied, "Do not allow the exposition of your private parts before anyone except your wife and slave-girl." I said, "O Messenger of Allah (S.A.W.) ! When people are mixed up and the man has no control over it, what should he do ?" He (S.A.W.) replied, "Try to keep your private parts concealed." I said, "O

Messenger of Allah (S.A.W.) ! Can a man not become naked when he is alone?" He (S.A.W.) replied, "Allah is Omnipresent and the man should be more *ashamed* before him than the people." *(Tirmizi, Ibn Majah).*

'Utba-bin Abdus Salma relates the Holy Prophet (S.A.W.) said, "When anyone from amongst you wishes to have sexual intercourse with his wife, he should cover himself and in this state they must not become naked like donkeys." *(Ibn-Majah)*

This teaching has raised moral standard of man in the society. It is a model for the people to follow in the modern world, if they really want clean and evil-free society for their peace, tranquility and happiness. The beloved wife of the Holy Prophet (S.A.W.), Hazrat Ayeshah (R.A.A.) says, "I never saw the parts of the body of the Holy Prophet (S.A.W.)."

This is the standard of honour and dignity in Islam. It does not permit nudity and shamelessness under any circumstances. Shamelessness is not allowed even in the affairs which are lawful. Whereas in the Western world nudity and shamelessness have become very common. How can a person remain good in a society where evil is rampant ?

Final Accountability

Modesty is a natural instinct of man but his adherence to it depends upon the fear of accountability on the Day of Judgment. Otherwise, there is always possibility of its being neglected. The fear of disgrace helps a person to sustain his modesty. If there is no fear of disgrace, he can subject himself to any shameful and sinful act.

Islam creates the feeling in human heart that there is a Supreme Power from Whom nothing remains hidden. Whatever man does in the day or night, the Supreme Power knows it, and the Day is sure to come when every person shall be accountable to Allah. Therefore, the very thought of the Hereafter keeps man away from all evils. The man who realises that he has to submit the account of his life to Allah on the Day of Judgment, he cannot commit sins. The Holy Quran discusses about the Day of Judgment at various places and reminds a believer to keep away from evil. The Holy Quran also promises rewards in the Hereafter for the virtuous and pious person.

The Holy Quran repeats the same matter in detail in these verses :

On that day faces will be bright as dawn,
laughing, rejoicing at good news;
And other faces, on that day, with dust upon them,
Veiled in darkness,
Those are the disbelievers, the wicked. (80 : 38-42)

"For those who do good is the best (reward) and more (thereto). Neither dust nor ignominy cometh near their faces. Such are rightful owners of the Garden; they will abide therein. And those who earn ill deeds (for them) requital of each ill deed by the like thereof; and ignominy overtaketh them—They have no protection from Allah—as if their faces had been covered with a cloak of darkest night. Such are rightful owners of the Fire; they will abide therein. (10 : 27-28)

It will be worthwhile to cite an incident from the life of Hazrat Yusuf (A.S.). While in prison in Egypt, he was approached by the most beautiful women of Egyptian royal court and invited to have an affair with them, and not only be freed from imprisonment, but lead an easy life in the royal court. But the heart of Hazrat Yusuf was full of the fear of Allah and he had a hope to see His Vision on the Day of Judgment, and as such he could not be bewitched by these damsels. The Prophet however, prays to Allah seeking His help in thwarting the attempts of these women to seduce him, thus :

"O my Lord ! Prison is more dear than that unto which they urge me, and if Thou fend not off their viles from me I shall incline unto them and become of the foolish." (12 : 33)

It is an asset of the Muslim to have faith in Allah and the Day of Judgment. This faith shields him from the attack of all vices. It is the faith that keeps a believer firm and fearless in life. He prays to Allah in all the difficulties of his life.

There is a lot of difference in thinking. On one side different tactics are used for the satisfaction of sexual desire, the ways and means of deception are created all around and all possible methods are used to destroy piety and virtue. On the other hand, the man of same blood and flesh, keeps away from all such temptations. He prefers to lead a hard life than to indulge in evil practices and thus earn ill-fame. He does all this because his heart is filled with faith in Allah.

Another example is that of Hazrat Mariam, the mother of Christ. One day all of a sudden a handsome person with proportionate limbs appears before her she screams with fear and invokes Allah's helps and says :

> "Lo ! I seek refuge in the Beneficent One from thee, if thou ant God-fearing." (19 : 18)

When that person told her that he was an angel in human form and that he had come to give happy tidings of the birth of a baby, to her. She was astonished to hear this and asked him :

> "How can I have a son when no mortal hath touched me, neither have I been unchaste." (19 : 20)

The Holy Prophet (S.A.W.) has said :

"There are seven types of men who will be sheltered by Allah on the Day when there shall be no other shelter. These include, the youth who is brought up in the environment of devotion to Allah; it includes a man who rejects the offer of dignified and pretty woman to have illicit relation with her saying that he fears Allah, and it includes a man who prays to Allah unostentatiously and in solitude his eyes get filled with tears of repentance when he thinks of his deeds."

(Bukhari - Muslim)

This high character is developed through the fear of the Day of Judgment and Islam expects every Muslim to possess such noble character.

Concept of Sin in Islam

Islam has presented a distinct picture of good and evil so that a Muslim may not go astray from the right path. The study of Islam equips him with the knowledge of understanding what is right and what is wrong. So finally he succeeds in keeping himself off from all evils. The Holy Quran is the best and the only guidance for mankind. Every act which is against the injunctions of the Holy Quran is a sin. The Holy Quran has explained thoroughly the grave sins.

As regards the sexual urge in human beings, the Holy Quran has declared in unequivocal terms that it is a measure to test their virtues and evil instincts. The immense attraction or sex appeal to male or female for the opposite sex, is a situation when it can be ascertained as to whether he or she is a virtuous person or one given to voluptuousness. On the one hand are his or her carnal or sensual urges which make him or her determined to violate each and every restriction in his or her way to accomplish the epicurian desire, and on the other, the fear of Allah, wisdom, decency and morality. This dilemma becomes a touch-stone for a person's claim to be virtuous and one with faith. The Holy Prophet has said."

"I have left behind me no evil more harmful to men than women." *(Bukhari)*

On another occasion the Holy Prophet (S.A.W.) has said :

> "Every morning two angels declare that men are source of destruction for women and women are destruction for men." *(Ibn Majah)*

Reward of Modesty

There are two ways for a man to protect himself from the curse of adultery and its consequences. Firstly he must not have any charm or liking for evil doing and secondly he must have proper means for the satisfaction of his sexual desires. The right ways must be made fascinating and attractive so that he may not go astray.

The way of life that Islam presents is more attractive and fascinating than wrong ways. Only the wicked take delight in evil and not the wise men, because Islam provides lawful means for the satisfaction of sexual desire. It emphasises moderation and modesty in life, the rewards of which is a graceful and well-balanced manner of life in this world and a contented life in the Hereafter. It promises *houris* living in Heaven for the righteous men.

What is the importance of worldly beauty before the heavenly beauty? It loses all its charm and attraction. The heavenly pleasure is pristine pure and eternal. The promise of this eternal beauty and charm makes the men righteous and pious in this world. He wants the real reward for his just milieu and modesty. And even in this world, there is no need to follow the evil ways for sexual pleasure, because Islam provides lawful means for the same.

Aim of Nikah (Marriage)

In order to uproot the causes of adultery, Islam has simplified the lawful means of sexual pleasure. The aim of marriage is to make the life of man lawful and modest which may make human life truly happy and prosperous. The *Nikah* shuts the door for adultery which is unnatural and mischievous, and its consequences are also disastrous. The Holy Quran says :

> "And whoso is not able to afford to marry free, believing women, let them marry from the believing maids whom your right hands possess. Allah knoweth best (covering) your faith. Ye (proceed) one from another; so wed them by permission of their folk and give unto them their portions in kindness, they being honest not debauched nor of loose conduct. And if when they are honourably married then commit lewdness they shall

'incur the half of the punishment (prescribed) for free women (in that case). This is for him among you who feareth to commit sin. But to have patience would be better for you. Allah is Forgiving, Merciful. (4 : 25)

In order to perform *Nikah* with a Muslim woman, a Muslim man has to keep in mind the four basic principles of Islam. Firstly, there must be mutual and free acceptance by both. Secondly there must be *Mehr* or dower money to offer to the woman to be wedded. Thirdly, the *Nikah* is to be performed strictly in accordance with the injunction of the Holy Quran and precept of the *Sunnah* of the Holy Prophet (S.A.W.). Fourthly there must be witnesses; two men or one man and two women and the *Nikah* should be performed in the presence of all the concerned persons.

The Holy Quran says :
"So wed them by permission of their folk, and give unto them their portions in kindness, they being honest, not debouched nor of loose conduct." (4 : 25)

Islam also permits a Muslim man to marry a women of the people of the Book. The Holy Quran says :
"This day are (all) good things made lawful for you. The food of those who have received the Scripture is lawful for you, and your food is lawful for them. And so are the virtuous women of the believers and the Virtuous women of those who received the Scripture before you (lawful for you) when ye give them their marriage portion and live with them in honour, not in fornication, nor taking them as secret concubnines." (5 : 5)

Uncontrolled sexual pleasure is like the flowing water which has no check in its way. It brings destructions for mankind. Hence Islam has laid down certain principles for the control of unchecked desires. The Islamic marriage controls the harmful ways of. sexual satisfaction and gives reward for the modesty. The other word for *Nikah* is *Aihsan. Hisn*' means the protected fort, a fine horse or a weapon.

These meanings show that the man is prevented from indulging in unlawful practices through *Nikah*. In other words, he is armed with such weapons which guard him against vicious sexual attacks.

The Holy Prophet (S.A.W.) has said :

"When any one of you comes across a woman--very attractive--and his heart is inclined towards her, he should go to his wife and have sexual intercourse with her so that he may keep himself away from such evil thoughts." *(Muslim--Tirmizi)*

This *Hadis* explicitly explains the aim of *Nikah*. *Nikah* is the commandment of Allah. It is, therefore, the must for every adult Muslim. It fulfils his desire and also saves him from all evils. He leads a respectable life and earns the pleasure of Allah.

Co-operation Between Husband and Wife.

The Islamic *Shariah* insists on co-operation between husband and wife for the achievement of the object of marriage. None of them should act in a manner injurious and harmful to their conjugal life. *Nikah* is the sacred tie between husband and wife. They have to love each other with sincerity and devotion without which none of them can attain peace of mind, progress and prosperity in social life. The Holy Quran says :

"And of His signs is this : He created for you helpmates from yourselves that ye might find rest in them, and He ordained between you love and mercy. Lo ! Herein indeed are portents for folk who reflect." (30 : 21)

Abu Hurairah (R.A.A.) relates that the Holy Prophet (S.A.W.) has said :

"When a husband calls upon his wife for sexual intercourse, and if she refuses and the husband remains angry the whole night, then the angels curse her until the morning." *(Bukhari, Muslim, and Abu Dawood)*

On another occasion the Holy Prophet (S.A.W.) has said:

"When a husband calls his wife for sexual intercourse, she must go at once, even if she may be busy in cooking." *(Tirmizi)*

Islam commands not only the women but also the men in this respect. It requires that the husband must always be aware of the feelings of his wife, otherwise he would be committing sin by depriving her of her rights. Abdur Rahman Al Jazari says :

"According to all four jurists of Islam, it is incumbent upon the husband to keep his wife happy and pleased in the best possible way. Likewise it is essential for the wife to satisfy the desire of the husband if he so wishes and she should not reject it unless there is some lawful excuse."

(Al Fiqh Alal Mazahib-il-Arba)

During a sermon, Hazrat 'Umar Farooq (R.A.A.) said :

"Protect the private parts of women."

(Musnand Ahmed)

This means it is essential for a husband to fulfil the desire of his wife in order to save her from following the wrong path.

Imam Ibn Taimiyah (R.A.) says, "It is very important right of the wife more important than her maintenance."

During the age of Ignorance in Arabia, sometimes a husband used to deprive his wife of her conjugal rights. Hence she could not satisfy her sexual desire, despite the fact that she had her husband. This act of the husband opened the door to evil practices in the society. Islam has forbidden all such practices which lead to evil ways.

Islam has decreed unlawful to commit sodomy with the wife because it is unnatural and deprives her of her right of sexual satisfaction. Hazrat Abu Hurairah (R.A.) relates that the Holy Prophet (S.A.W.) has said :

"Be curse of Allah upon the husband who commits sodomy with his wife." *(Abu Dawood)*

There is another narration by Hazrat Abu Hurairah :

> "The Holy Prophet (S.A.W.) said ! "Allah will not see the face of the man who has committed sodomy with his wife." *(Ibn Majah)*

Explaining this *Hadis* Imam Ibn Qayyim says :

"It is the right of the wife that her husband should have natural way of sexual relation. By committing sodomy or unnatural intercourse with her, he deprives her of her right and also fails to satisfy her sexual desire. Nor the purpose of having a wife is served. Besides, she has not been created for this dirty act. Hence all those who avoid the natural course and indulge in unnatural means, ignore the wisdom of Allah and His *Shariah.*" *(Zadul Ma'ad)*

This strict order is not without reason. The purpose of *Nikah* would be lost if the spouses fail to ward off the evils of sexual relation. Therefore, *Nikah* has been made the source of the protection of chastity.

Love is the basis of sexual relation between husband and wife. Without this the spouses cannot give that amount of satisfaction and pleasure to each other, which is required by nature. Those men and women who fall in love with each other must marry. The Holy Prophet (S.A.W.) has said :

> "There is no better way for the two persons, loving each other, than to marry." *(Ibn Majah)*

There are two aspects of this *Hadis*. The one is that if there exists natural and genuine love between two persons, it is proper for them to marry each other so that they may not go astray and become harmful to the society, instead they may prove an asset to the society. Secondly, harmony in nature helps in the protection of chastity. Because when a man loves through lawful means, his attention will hardly be diverted towards the unlawful means.

The difference in the ages of husband and wife is also a factor in developing charm in legitimate relations; disparity in age creates bitterness in conjugal life. Therefore, according to Islam there should not be much difference in the ages of the couple. There are two instances in support of this argument. Hazrat Jabir (R.A.A.) married a widow in his youth, so the Holy Prophet (S.A.W.) asked :

"Why did you not marry a young woman so that both of you could have enjoyed the conjugal life better." *(Bukhari)*

Hazrat Abu Bakr (R.A.A.) and Hazrat 'Umar (R.A.A.) requested the Holy Prophet (S.A.W.) for the hand of Hazrat Fatimah (R.A.A.), but he (S.A.W.) rejected their request on the ground that she was younger in age. However, when Hazrat Ali (R.A.A.) requested for his marriage with her, the Holy Prophet (S.A.W.) accepted the offer and her *Nikah* was performed with him. It is also said that Holy Prophet (S.A.W.) himself had made this offer to Hazrat Ali (R.A.A.).

Imam Nasai has said, "It is suitable and noble for a woman to marry a man of her age." *(Sunnan).* This stand is quite in accordance with the principles of Islamic *Shariah.*

Islamic *Shariah* also permits the man to see the women for the purpose of *Nikah.* This facilitates him to deceide whether the contemplated *Nikah* would be suitable or not. Mughirah-bin-Sh'oba relates that when he proposed to marry a woman the Holy Prophet (S.A.W.) said :

"Go and see her (first) because it is good in order to have harmonious relation." *(Tirmizi)*

This *Hadis* shows that the *Shariah* wants true love between husband and wife for a successful and lasting conjugal life and there may not be anything which may cause disharmony between them and may create a chance for some sort of mischief.

Islam allows the wife to make herself up and wear decent dresses for the pleasure of herself and her husband. But it forbids her to exhibit herself before strangers, because in the first case it strengthens the union of the spouses whereas in the second case, it does not allow her to appear fully decorated before a stranger. In the first instance, it is intended to generate in her husband attraction for her, and in the second, this attraction is subdued.

In the early days of the Islamic history, women beautified themselves for the sake of their husbands. Once Hazrat Ayeshah (R.A.A.) found the wife of Usman bin Maz'oon unadorned as against the traditions of the time. She at once asked her, "Has Usman (R.A.A.) gone out on journey?"
(Musnad Ahmad)

Expounding this *Hadis* Imam Shokani (R.A.) says :

"Hazrat Ayeshah's (R.A.A.) surprise over giving up hair dying and use of scent, shows that it is a good thing for the wives to adorn themselves for the pleasure of their husbands..
(Nail Autar)

On another occasion, the Holy Prophet (S.A.W.) said that when a man returns from a journey, he should not enter the house unannounced or suddenly, because he may see any member of the family in such a state that he may not like.

Hazrat Jabir (R.A.A.) says that they had returned from a battle and wanted to go to their houses when the Holy Prophet (S.A.W.) said :

"Sit tight, and enter your houses at night, so that the woman who has not dressed up may get time to smarten herself and one whose husband was away, may take bath and become neat and clean." *(Bukhari)*

Islam respects the sentiments of both males and females. According to Islam woman is not just the means of sexual satisfaction, or merely a lump of flesh without emotions and feelings. On the contrary her heart is the abode of delicate sensations. Rough manners and crudeness may hurt her feelings. Therefore, the husband has to be very cautious and he should not act in a manner which may be unpalatable to her temperament. He should treat her with love and tenderness. The Holy Prophet (S.A.W.) has said :

> "Woman is like a rib. If you try to straighten it, it will break. And if you leave it as it is, you will get pleasure inspite of its being crooked." *(Bukhari–Muslim)*

On another occasion the Holy Prophet (S.A.W.) has said, "It should not happen that any one of you beats his wife like a slave and then sleep with her at night." *(Bukhari)*

Abdullah-bin-Abbas (R.A.A.) says that he likes to be well dressed and decent to his wife, as he himself expects his wife to be adorned and well-dressed. *(Sunan-ul-Kubra)*

Islam also teaches the spouses to be above board morally because it is one of the essentials of happy and harmonious conjugal life. The life and character of the Holy Prophet (S.A.W.) is the best model for every husband of the world to follow and practise in respect of the conjugal life.

Once the Holy Prophet (S.A.W.) related an interesting story of eleven women. Most of them had complained against their husbands. But the eleventh one, Umme Zara said, "I have no words to praise my husband. He has covered my ears with ornaments, and fed me so well that my lean and thin arms have become plumpy. In short, he has provided me with everything to keep me happy and I am happy. I am very lucky. I lived in an ordinary family of shepherds; now he has settled me in a house of people possessing horses and camels and doing cultivation. I talk to him freely and frankly but he never objects. I sleep comfortably till morning and eat delicious food."

Then the Holy Prophet (S.A.W.) said to Hazrat Ayeshah, "I am like Abu Zara for you."

Once Hazrat Ayeshah (R.A.A.) related an interesting parable to the Holy Prophet (S.A.W.) and asked, "O Messenger of Allah (R.A.A.) tell me : While passing through a wooded valley would you (S.A.W.) prefer to graze your goats near a tree with leaves or under a tree without leaves?" The Holy Prophet (S.A.W.) replied, "I would have grazed my goats near the tree full of leaves." *(Bukhari)*

All wives of the Holy Prophet (S.A.W.) were widows except Hazrat Ayeshah (R.A.A.) who was a spinster when the Holy Prophet (S.A.W.) married her.

According to a famous narration some Negroes were displaying the gymnastic games on the Eid day. The Holy Prophet (S.A.W.) asked Hazrat Ayeshah (R.A.A.) "Would you like to watch this show?" When she said, "Yes", the Holy Prophet (S.A.W.) asked her to stand behind him. When she got tired, the Holy Prophet (S.A.W.) said, "Then go now." *(Bukhari—Muslim)*

Hazrat Ayeshah (R.A.A.) says, "After having eaten some part of the meat on the bone, I used to give it to the Holy Prophet (S.A.W.) who (S.A.W.) would bite the morsel from the place where I had bitten. Similarly when I used to offer some beverage after drinking a part, he (S.A.W.) would drink from the side, I drank." *(Muslim)*

There are numerous instances of this kind which prove that Islam permits making conjugal life happy and colourful.

CHAPTER 15

PRECAUTIONARY MEASURES

Control of Eyes

Allah has endowed mankind with charm and beauty. Mankind is also fond of beautiful things. Therefore, man seeks beauty in every thing of the world. He despises ugly and awkward things and he is never tired of seeking beauty in the Nature.

Indeed, it is natural urge of mankind, hence it is essential to fulfil it. But this admiration of beauty is worthwhile so long it is within the limits of *Shariah*. If it crosses the limits then it opens the door to evil practices which spoil the society. Therefore, Islam restricts the observation of the opposite sex, because, if the sight is not controlled, then it will be difficult to control the sexual desire.

> The Holy Quran says :
> "Say to the believing men that they should lower their gaze and guard their modesty that will make far greater purity for them and Allah is well acquainted with all that they do. And say to the believing women that they should also lower their gaze and guard their modesty."
> (24 : 30-31)

According to the Holy Quran, it is necessary for a man to control his eyes to keep his character blameless. The Holy Prophet (S.A.W.) has said :

> "O Ali ! Do not have a second look—the first glance may be by chance, but the second view is not justified."
> *(Abu Dawood — Tirmizi)*

This *Hadis* means that the first (casual) sight is pardonable, but the second and deliberate looking is not proper because they are Satanic acts which destroy the human character. Hazrat Jabir-bin-Abdullah says, "I asked the Holy Prophet (S.A.W.) if I happen to look at the stranger by chance what should be done?" The Holy Prophet (S.A.W.) replied, "Turn your face at once.

(Muslim-Tirmizi-Abu Dawood)

Control on Hearing

Hearing also leaves profound impression on human feelings and emotions. This impression can be harmful or beneficial. It is the aim of the good law to clarify the lines of loss and gain. Hence, Islam lays down the rule that a Muslim can hear any beautiful song for the satisfaction of his interest. However, it prohibits the kind of hearing which leads to sexual incitement and immorality, because Islam wants a man to be of finest character. There is nothing wrong in listening to sweet melody but it is a sin to listen to anything that is morally harmful. Therefore, music or musical instruments are not allowed in Islam. The reason for the ban is explained in the best way by Hafiz Ibn Jauzi (R.A.) :

"It should be known that there are two kinds of harms in listening to the music; the one is that it makes man negligent in his duty towards Allah, and secondly it inclines his thinking towards the worldly pleasures only. He strives to satisfy his material wants only particularly the sexual desire which is on the top. And it is not possible to satisfy these wants without having new contact. Such possibilities could not be found in the lawful area of life. Music also incites man for unlawful sexual pleasure. If music is the food of soul, the sexual pleasure is the food of the body. It is related in a *Hadis* that music leads to sexual pleasure."

(Naqdul Ilm-wal-Ulema)

The Control of the Tongue

The man has been proved very careless in respect of the use of his tongue. Whatever a man utters, it effects the people and the environment. The effects of the tongue are stronger than those of seeing and hearing. The tongue is the means of expression of human thoughts which may be good or bad and accordingly these thoughts leave their impression on the people around. The speaker tries to influence the listener with his power of the tongue. If his speech is liked and appreciated by the listeners then his thoughts grow stronger and this process leads to collective listening and thus his influence grows stronger day by day.

The fact cannot be denied that the power of speech can create chaos if not controlled and allowed to be used wrongly. Hazrat Sohail bin Sa'd relates that the Holy Prophet (S.A.W.) has said :

> "If a person gives me guarantee for the protection of (his or her) tongue and sexual organs, I shall guarantee Heaven for him (or) (her)." *(Bukhari)*

On another occasion the Holy Prophet (S.A.W.) said :

> "A person who is saved from the evil of the tongue by Allah, shall enter Heaven." *(Tirmizi)*

Dress

Today the greatest evil of the world is the nudism, which has greatly influenced the human mind and provided the unlimited means of sensuality. The fair sex is already attractive and charming in appearance and if nudity is added, the mischief is greater, making it difficult for the man to control his passions. Therefore, Islam condemns all means and sources of evil which lead to immorality and destroy the human society. The purpose of clothing is to ward off the evil consequences of nudity and maintain decency in the society.

It is the sign of utter ignorance to think that nudity is the call of modernization. In fact, the nudism is the imitation of Western culture. It has nothing to do with the term, 'Modern.' Islam is the most modern '*Deen*'. It, not only allows the advancement in modern science and technology but also encourages all efforts intended to attain knowledge from any part of the world.

The concept of dress in Islam is to cover the body, specially those parts, which must not be exposed to others. It also emphasises decency in dressing. Therefore, Islam has given certain guidelines for the dresses of the man and the woman and both have to follow these instructions strictly. Hazrat Ayeshah (R.A.A.) says that she has heard the Holy Prophet (S.A.W.) saying :

> "A woman who removes her clothes in a house other than that of her husband, violates the command of Allah." *(Musnad Ahmad)*

Prohibition of a Woman Being Alone in the Company of Stranger

It is a very dangerous idea for a woman to meet a stranger in loneliness. Logically speaking, there is no sense in meeting a stranger when a woman has no relation with a man. In such circumstances she cannot be sure of protecting her chastity from the attack of the stranger. Therefore Islam strictly prohibits woman from meeting a stranger in loneliness. This is done for her own safety and protection of her honour. Hazrat Jabir (R.A.A.) relates that the Holy Prophet (S.A.W.) has said :

> "The women who have no company of their near relatives, should not visit strangers, because nobody knows when the devil inside man incites him for the commission of sin." *(Muslim—Tirmizi)*

CHAPTER 16

THE SOCIAL REFORM

The Basic Principles

There are certain principles which are to be followed by the individuals in the society. No society can allow the opposition or rejection of the principles, because the non-compliance amounts to rebellion against the society. If any society gives up these principles or fails to enforce them, it will disintegrate.

The Islamic society has its own principles which must be followed by the Muslims. The requirements of these principles are explained by the Holy Quran at various places. At one place it says :

> "O mankind ! Be careful of your duty to your Lord who created you from a single soul and from it created its mate and from them twain hath spread abroad a multitude of men and women. Be careful of your duty toward Allah in Whom ye claim (your rights) of one another, and toward the wombs (that base you).
>
> Lo ! Allah hath been a Watcher over you." (4 : 1)
>
> "O Prophet, when believing women come to thee to take oath of fidelity, that they will not associate in worship any other thing whatever, with Allah, that they will not resort to stealing, that they will not commit fornication, that they will not kill their children, that they will not utter slanders intentionally forging falsehood, and that they will not disobey thee in any just matter, then do thou receive their fidelity, and

> pray to Allah for the forgiveness (of their sins) for Allah is Oft-forgiving, Most Merciful." (60 : 12)

The principles are meant for the women because, when the Islamic society was developing in Madina, the Islamic State had entered into a treaty with the people of Mecca, on account of certain diplomatic considerations, undertaking not to give shelter to any of the Quraish against their wish. The Muslims could afford asylum to only such women who wanted it. In this background, the Holy Quran has explained the conditions to be followed by a woman in order to become a part of the Islamic society. However, the Muslim men are no exception to these rules. Hazrat Ubada-bin-Samit (R.A.A.) says :

> "The Holy Prophet (S.A.W.) had taken oath from us similar to those of women, that we must not believe in plurality of God, nor steal, nor commit adultery, nor commit infanticide, nor blame each other." *(Muslim)*

This statement of oath clearly explains the concept of Islamic society. It also explains the aims and objects of Islam in respect of the human society. There is no place for the people other than those who are good and virtuous. It is but natural that a good society cannot permit unhealthy environment within itself.

The Quran says :

> "We also sent Lot. He said to His people; Do ye commit lewdness such as no people have so far committed before you? For ye practise your lusts on men in preference to women : Ye are indeed a people transgressing beyond bounds. And his people gave no answer but this : They said, "Drive them out of your city : These are indeed men who want to be clean and pure." (7 : 80-82)

If a man thinks that evil practices are destructive to the mankind, he has to change the present criminal environment and make the society free from evil.

One of the most important facts is that though there are rules in all societies for the prevention of evil, the failure of implementation is seen everywhere. It is not possible to have a good society unless the laws are strictly implemented and followed.

The distinct characteristics of Islam is that it creates a refined society. It becomes incumbent upon every Muslim to follow the principles of Islam strictly in order to make his own life safe and respectable. It is not possible to lead a peaceful and respectable life without adhering to the principles prescribed by the *Shariah*.

The Force of Ideology

For the enforcement of an ideology, a society must have three powers : The force of ideology, the force of collective thinking and feeling and the force of law. The force of Islamic ideology is the only capable force to wipe out the evil from the surface of the earth and establish a pious society all over the world. The other ideologies have failed because they are man-made and devoid of Natural laws. The world has tried all possible laws made by man and achieved nothing. On the contrary there prevails distrubance and uneasiness. Therefore, the world has no other alternative but to adopt Islamic laws for the peace and good of mankind.

The man-made laws demand the obedience to the man in authority. Therefore, the people easily ignore these laws and indulge in evil practices. Besides, these laws fail to punish and change the offenders. Whereas, the laws of Islam demand the obedience to Allah, the Creator of all. It is the fear of Allah that keeps man away from the evil practices. The man, who loves Allah, would never like to displease Almighty Allah. The Holy Quran says :

> "Eschew all sins, open or secret : Those who earn sin will get due recompense for their Earnings." (6 : 120)

At other place, the Holy Quran says :

"Say : the things that my Lord hath indeed forbidden are shameful deeds, whether open or secret." (7 : 33)

Islam does not permit any kind of evil under any circumstances. Moreover, the Islamic law cannot be changed by man because he has no authority to do so. Islam disbands the jungle law and enforces the law of Islamic *Shariah* for the establishment of good and refined society. Islam makes the man and the woman morally high and cultured.

It is a fact that woman can live honourably and peacefully only if the society is good, and good society is possible only if its members are good. Suleman bin Baridah (R.A.A.) relates from his father that the Holy Prophet (S.A.W.) has said :

"Those men who do not go to the battlefield for *Jihad* and remain at home, for them the wives of the *Mujahideen* are as respectable as their own mothers. If a man from amongst the people who have stayed at home happens to be the custodian of a *Mujahid* and if he misappropriates, he shall be brought before the *Mujahideen* on the Day of Judgment and he would take away as much good deeds from him as he would like. Just imagine, what would be the condition of that culprit." *(Muslim, Abu Dawood)*

Zaid-bin-Khalid (R.A.A.) relates that the Holy Prophet (S.A.W.) said :

"A man who provided arms to a *Mujahid*, he got the reward of *Jihad*. And the man who looked after the family of the *Mujahid*, too earned the reward of *Jihad*." *(Bukhari, Muslim)*

The Moral Values

Undcubtedly, the society which is based on such lofty ideals and piety, gives prime importance to moral values. Such a society is the noblest in the world. The men and the women of such a society bear high moral character, and such is the Muslim society. The moral values help men and women to ward off evil and lead virtuous life. In this Islamic society, the individuals respect each other and never become hurdle in any way. The man, who possesses high moral character, is an asset for the society because he not only himself remains good but also helps in the prevention of evils in the society. He has great regard, specially, for the women. The moral values also make the human conscience strong.

> "Who so obeyeth Allah and His Messenger, He will make him enter gardens underneath which rivers flow, where such will dwell for ever. That will be the great success." (4 : 13)

> "And whoso disobeyeth Allah and His Messenger, and transgresseth His limits, He will make him enter Fire, where such will dwell for ever; his will be a shameful doom." (4 : 14)

Imam Ibne Taimiyah (R.A.) says :

"If a person is forced to commit fornication, it is incumbent upon him or her to resist. If the attacker runs away, then it is well and good. If not, then the attacker's life can be taken which is in accordance with the unanimous view of the jurists." *(Mukhtarat-e-Islamiyah)*

Islam considers it a human right to protect one's honour. Therefore, it gives no authority to any person to violate the chastity of any woman or dishonour her. It also forbids false accusation against a woman. The Holy Quran says :

> "And those who level false allegation of adultery against a chaste woman and fail to produce four witnesses (to support their allegation), flog them with eighty stripes and reject their evidence for ever, for such men are wicked transgressors." (24 : 4)

The Wicked Are Condemned

On the one hand, Islam considers it unlawful to falsely defame an innocent woman; this is done in order to enable her to live honourably. On the other hand, Islam condemns the wicked people specially bad characters. Such bad characters are not accorded a decent position in Islamic society as that of virtuous men and women. They always lead disgraceful life. Only the western society harbours such ruffians but there is no place for them in the Islamic society. In fact a bad character cannot survive in Islamic society. As the Holy Quran says :

> "Let no man guilty of adultery or fornication marry any but a woman similarly guilty, or an unbeliever. Nor let any but such a man or an unbeliever marry such a woman. To the believers such a thing is fobidden."
>
> (24 : 3)

Hazrat Abu Hurairah and Zaid-bin-Khalid (R.A.A.) relate that the Holy Prophet (S.A.W.) was asked what should be done with an unmarried slave-girl who commits adultery? The Holy Prophet (S.A.W.) replied, "If she commits adultery, she must be lashed, if she commits adultery again, then lash her again; and if she still commits adultery then lash her and then sell her off even at the cost of a rope."

(Bukhari)

Islam Forbids Celibacy

In Islam there is no place for celibacy. If a person is poor, it is the duty of the other well-to-do Muslims to help that person to get married. This is the only way to save that person from immorality and enable him or her to lead a respectable life in the society. According to the Holy Quran it is the natural right of the person.

> "Marry those among you who are single, or the virtuous ones among your slaves, male or female." (24 : 32)

The demand of this verse is that no one should remain unmarried in the Islamic society so that the sexual desire may not lead one to unlawful means. This command applies to all Muslim men and women whether free or slave. The Islamic

Society of the early era made all necessary arrangements for the marriage of deserving persons to fulfil the conditions of the *Shariah*.

A well-known *'Tabie* or companion of the companions, Ahnaf (R.A.) says that there are three matters which cannot be delayed. When he was asked to name those matters, he said, "The performance of good deed, the burial of the dead and the marriage of a virgin." He has also said, "He would prefer to have the presence of a python in a corner of his house than to refuse the proposal of marriage from a man of equal age for an unmarried girl." *(Al Bayan Wat Tibiyan)*

Shaddad bin Aus (R.A.A.) said to his relatives, "Make the arrangement for my marriage because the Holy Prophet (S.A.W.) has advised me not to meet my Allah without marriage." *(Al Ahkam-ul-Quran)*

Mujahid (R.A.) relates that Abdullah bin Abbas (R.A.A.) used to tell his slaves, "If any one of you wants to marry, I can arrange. Remember, there is a possibility of indulgence in adultery if you remain celibate. And Allah takes away the faith *(Iman)* from the man who commits adultery. Then it is left to Allah whether to return the faith to him or not." *(Al Muhalla Ibn Hazm)*

Imam Nakhayee says, "The masters used to force their slaves to marry and if they refused, they were locked in the houses." *(Tafseer Qurtubi)*

They were locked up so that they may not be the cause of evil in the society. It is not only an individual who is responsible in the society but it is also the duty of the state to make the necessary arrangement for marriage of the people who cannot afford.

The Holy Prophet (S.A.W.) has said :

"The ruler of the time is the guardian of the woman who is helpless." *(Tirmizi, Abu Dawood)*

The Holy Prophet (S.A.W.) had asked Hazrat Ali to remember three things :

> "Offer the prayers in time; if somebody dies, do not delay the burial; and if an unmarried person finds a suitable match then arrange the marriage immediately."
> *(Tirmizi)*

In reply to the Governor of Koofa Zaid-bin-Abdur Rehman, Hazrat 'Umar-bin-Abdul Aziz (R.A.) says, "You have written that there is surplus money even after paying the salaries to the army. Then pay the debts of the debtors and the amount of the dower of those who are unable to pay." *(Seerat Umar bin Abdul Aziz)*

Permission for the Marriage of Four Wives

Sexual feelings exist in a man upto a certain period of the age but the life of woman repeatedly passes through such stages when her emotions become weak and sometimes this state continues for a long period; therefore she cannot adequately fulfil the sexual demands of her husband. It is for this reason, Islam has allowed man to marry four wives. Thus Islam prevents him from going astray. However, if he has four wives at a time, he has to do justice and treat them equally because the Holy Quran says :

> "Marry women of your choice, two or three or four, but if ye fear that ye shall not be able to deal justly (with them), then only one, or a captive." (4 : 3)

> "Ye will not be able to deal equally between (your) wives, however much ye wish (to do so). But turn not altogether away (from one), leaving her as in suspense."
> (4 : 129)

Thus it is crystal clear that Islam grants a conditional permission to marry upto four wives and not a licence. Islam is the natural religion hence the Quranic injunctions are also based on human nature.

The Holy Quran claims :

"O ye who believe ! Be ye staunch in justice, witnesses for Allah, even though it be against yourselves or (your) parents or (your) kindred, whether (the case be of) a rich man or a poor man, for Allah is nearer unto both (than ye are). So follow not passion lest ye lapse (from truth) and if he lapse or fall away, then lo ! Allah is ever informed of what ye do." (4 : 135)

The Holy Prophet (S.A.W.) remarks, "When a man has two wives and he does not observe equality and deal un-justly with them, he will come before the Throne of Justice of Allah with only half of his body." *(Bukhari)*

Allama Ibn Ilham Hanafi has explained the legality of this verse in these words : "This proves that a man can marry four wives only if there is no fear of injustice to them and if there is a fear, then no more than one wife is allowed. It is clear that in case of more than one wife, justice is essential." *(Fathul Qadeer)*

Allama Badruddin Kashani remarks :

"If a husband has two wives or two captives, then it is essential for him to maintain equality and justice between them as regards clothes, house and passing of the nights." *(Al Badae-was-Sanai)*

Woman's Right to Second Marriage

The physical conditions of the woman are different from those of the man. Therefore, Islam also enjoins strictly the marriage of the woman. And the stress is the same as that of the man. However, Islam does not permit the plurality of husbands for the woman, but has made the provision for the continuity of her conjugal life. It never deprives her of her legitimate right of sexual satisfaction. In case she is separated from her husband owing to his death or divorce, Islam lays stress upon her second marriage after the passage of the requisite period of *'iddat'*. The History of Islam shows that the second marriage of the women was performed very easily during the period of the Holy Prophet (S.A.W.) and the Khulafa-i-Rashideen (R.A.A.).

'Aatika-bint-Zaid was married to Hazrat Abu Bakr's (R.A.A.) son, Abdullah. Due to some reasons, Hazrat Abu Bakr (R.A.A.) advised his son to divorce his wife. Though, Abdullah divorced his wife to please his father but he was very sad because he loved her very much. When Hazrat Abu Bakr came to know of this fact, he gave his son permission to re-marry her. After the second marriage, Abdullah was martyred in the battle of *Taif*. It is related that Zaid-bin-Khattab married 'Aatika after the martyrdom of her husband. When he was also martyred in the battle of Yamama, Hazrat Umar (R.A.A.) married her. And after Hazrat 'Umar (R.A.A.), Hazrat Zubair (R.A.A.) married her. After his martyrdom, Hazrat Ali (R.A.A.) offered her to marry but she herself refused.

Sohaila-bint-Sohail married four companions of the Holy Prophet (S.A.W.) one after the other. Similarly, Jamila, the daughter of Abdullah-bin-Ubai was married to Hazrat Hanzla (R.A.A.). When he was martyred in the battle of Uhud, Sabit-bin-Qais married her. After him, Malik-bin-Wakhsham married her and after him she was married to Habib-bin-Liaf.

Asma bint Umais's first marriage was solemnized with Jafar (R.A.A.), the brother of Hazrat Ali (R.A.A.). After his death, Hazrat Abu Bakr (R.A.A.) married her. And after the death of Hazrat Abu Bakr (R.A.A.), Hazrat Ali (R.A.A.) married her.

Umme Kulsoom daughter of Hazrat Ali (R.A.A.) was married to Hazrat 'Umar (R.A.A.). When Hazrat 'Umar (R.A.A.) was martyred, Aun-bin-Jafer (R.A.A.) married her. After the death of Aun, his brother Abdullah married her. *(Tabaqat, Al Istiyab).*

These examples prove that the second marriage of the woman is not a matter of disgrace in Islam. It is done with respect and honour to keep the society clean and good.

The Right to Divorce

Islam permits divorce but not just like that. Not only that it is discouraged but also considered as the most abhorrent act. It is allowed in a situation when it becomes inevitable owing to the danger of violation of the limits prescribed by Allah.

When the lives of the husband and the wife turn into a hell, the Islamic law would not compel them to bind them-selves together for ever. When the confidence between them is shaken, it is better for them to separate.

In case of an extremely difficult situation, the Holy Quran says :

> "As for those who accuse their wives but have no witnesses except themselves; let the testimony of one of them be four testimonies, (swearing) by Allah that he is of those who speak the truth;
> And yet a fifth, invoking the curse of Allah on him if he is of those who lie.
> And it shall avert the punishment from her if she bear witness before Allah four times that the things he saith is indeed false. And fifth (time) that the wrath of Allah be upon her if he speaketh truth." (24 : 6-9)

The Holy Quran is the complete code of life. It deals with every aspect of human life. And divorce is one of the aspects. The law of divorce provides protection to human modesty and chastity.

The aim of marriage in Islam is to enable a person to lead virtuous life and to create healthy environments in the society. The marriage can be successful only if there is harmony between husband and wife. It is also essential that they must be capable to satisfy the sexual need of each other

Islam gives the full right to the spouses to divorce each other in case the other party lacks the capability for proper discharge of sexual functions. Hazrat 'Umar (R.A.A.), Hazrat Ali (R.A.A.) and other Companions opine that not only the sexual incapability but also the diseases like blindness, leprosy and lunacy are the valid grounds for divorce. However Imam Ibn Qayyim (R.A.) says :

"It is not enough to rely on Two, Six, Seven or Eight defects and neglect the other major or equal defects. The separation can take place on any ground that creates hatred between the spouses and the love is lost which is the sole aim of the marriage." *(Zad-ul-Muad)*

The Importance of Lawful Relation

On the one hand, Islam emphasises the discontinuation of the conjugal relation, which fails to fulfil the requirement of the marriage and on the other hand, it encourages the spouses to adhere to the bonds of marriage which help in leading a virtuous life. Unless there is love between the spouses and they satisfy the sexual wants of each other, the marriage cannot be successful. Besides, the strained relation leads to evil practices.

The marriage is considered a firm bond in the Islamic society. It is based on the natural wants of a man and a woman. Hence the sanctity of the *Nikah* cannot be violated under any circumstances. Though, Islam allows divorce but only on solid grounds. The marriage cannot be dissolved on trivial matters. The Holy Prophet (S.A.W.) has said :

"The women who seek divorce from their husbands without valid reasons are the hypocrites." *(Nasai)*

He (S.A.W.) has said on another occasion :

"The woman who seeks divorce from her husband without any solid ground, even the smell of Heaven is fobidden for her." *(Tirmizi)*

Yet on another occasion, the Holy Prophet (S.A.W.) has said :

"He is the greatest sinner before Allah who marries a woman and leaves her after satisfying his sexual desire and also swallows her dower." *(Mustadrak Hakim)*

It is the duty of an individual and also of the society to respect the lawful marriage. When the illegitimate relation is condemnable in Islam, the legitimate and lawful relation is respected. It is the duty of the whole society to respect the sanctity of solemn marriage. In Islam no one is permitted to violate the sanctity of marriage. According to the Holy Quran the married women are forbidden for the other men. The Holy Prophet (S.A.W.) has said :

"That man is not from amongst us who turns a woman rebellious against her husband or the slave against the master." *(Abu Dawood)*

Imam Ibn Taimiya (R.A.) has remarked :

If a man with an intention to marry someone's wife himself or get her married to another man, kills her husband, the law of Islam says that such a man must be deprived of the rights to marry her and it is immaterial whether she herself was involved in the conspiracy or not." *(Iqama-tul-Daleel)*

The Social Responsibility

It is but natural that an individual leaves his or her impressions on the society as a whole. The person of a good moral character leaves good impressions on the society and if the person happens to be of bad character he or she leaves bad influence on the society. Thus a good person helps in the establishment of a good society and a person of bad character spoils the good society. Therefore, it is not possible to have healthy environment and good society in the world unless every individual realises that it is his or her duty to protect the good character of the society.

Islam creates a sense of duty in an individual and reminds that he or she is the real architect of the good society. Moreover, it is not enough for an individual just to be good but it is also his or her duty to correct and improve others. An individual bearing good moral character plays an important role in the building of a good and healthy environment. Such an individual saves others from the moral degeneration. The Holy Prophet (S.A.W.) says :

> "Listen, everyone of you is a guardian and everyone of you shall be questioned about the people. The Caliph who is the ruler of the people is a guardian and he shall be questioned about his subjects. The man is the guardian of the members of his family and he shall be questioned about them. The wife is the guardian of her children and the members of her husband's family, and she shall be questioned about them. The slave is the guardian of his master's wealth and he shall be questioned about it. Listen again; Every one of you is a guardian and everyone of you shall be questioned about the (concerned) people." *(Bukhari)*

The pressure of the society is always strong. And if it remains strong, no one would dare to disobey its set principles. If overall environment of the society is bad then all sorts of evils would creep in and the situation would go beyond control and the moral values would die.

Islam keeps the sense of morality alive in the society, hence it would not tolerate any kind of immoral act of an individual. Once a woman, who had scented her clothes, was passing through a road. Hazrat Abu Hurairah (R.A.A.) saw her and asked, "Are you coming from the mosque?" She replied "Yes". He further asked, "Have you applied this perfume for going to the mosque?" She replied in affirmation. Then Hazrat Abu Hurairah (R.A.A.) scolded her and said that he has heard his beloved friend the Holy Prophet (S.A.W.) saying :

> "A woman who applies perfume and goes to the mosque, Allah accepts not her prayers unless she takes bath as in case of dirtiness." *(Abu Dawood)*

The Holy Prophet (S.A.W.) saw Umme Darda (R.A.A.) coming from the bath and directed her not to go again. He (S.A.W.) told her :

> "The woman who removes her clothes at the place other than her house, tears the curtain that exists between her and Allah."
> *(Musnad Ahmad)*

According to Islam, it is the duty of man to protect moral values of the people who are socially related to him. This responsibility becomes vital if relation is closer. The chastity of the relative and the woman-neighbour must be protected. Any violation in this respect would amount to unpardonable sin.

> Hazrat Abdullah bin Masood (R.A.A.) says that a man asked the Holy Prophet (S.A.W.), "Which is the greatest sin?" The Holy Prophet (S.A.W.) replied, "The greatest sin is to associate someone with Allah, Who alone created you." He asked, "Which is the lesser sin than this?" The Holy Prophet (S.A.W.) replied, "After that, the greatest sin is to take the life of your baby thinking that it will take away the part of livelihood (and you would starve)." He again asked, "Which is the greatest sin after these two." The Holy Prophet (S.A.W.) replied. "The adultery with your neighbour (woman)."
> *(Bukhari, Muslim and Mishkat)*

Once the Holy Prophet (S.A.W.) asked one of his companions, "What is your opinion about adultery?" The companion replied, "Allah and his Messenger (S.A.W.) have forbidden adultery and it shall remain forbidden until the Day of Judgment." The Holy Prophet (S.A.W.) said, "The adultery with ten women is lesser sin than the adultery committed with his neighbour's wife."

CHAPTER 17

THE ISLAMIC LAW

The Blood Relation

When the man is born, he sees his parents, brothers, sisters and other close relatives around him; this is his first environment in which he is brought up. He has to make no efforts for the achievement of this environment but the Nature provides him. If this environment is taken away from him, he would not be able to create such an environment which can serve him selflessly, participate in his joys and sorrows and be useful in the solution of the problems of his life. Therefore, the man always depends upon the closest environment provided by the Nature. This environment has taken the form of a sacred home and sincere and noble sentiments of love and respect are attached to it.

The home has given the man protection against the evils of immorality, because Islam has forbidden sexual relation with the close blood relations. Even the names of such relatives are clearly mentioned in the Holy Quran with whom sexual intercourse is forbidden. Thus Islam has eliminated all possibilities of man going astray.

Secret Relations Are Also Forbidden

Islam does not allow any kind of unlawful secret relation between man and woman. The only way allowed for sex between man and woman, is *Nikah* according to the Islamic *Shariah*. *Nikah* is natural and lawful, because it is the Commandment of Allah and the *Sunnah* of the Holy Prophet (S.A.W.). There is no alternative as the Holy Quran says :

"They should be chaste, not lustful, nor taking paramours when they are taken in wedlock." (4 : 25)

The man wants to keep the sexual relation secret so that he can avoid the pressure of the society and remain free from all moral restrictions laid down by it. He considers these restrictions laid down by it, a hurdle on the way of his lawless living. Therefore, Islam does not allow any secrecy in this respect and commands the solemnization of *Nikah.*

Once a case of *Nikah* was brought before Hazrat 'Umar Farooq (R.A.A.) in which the only witnesses were a man and a woman. Hazrat 'Umar remarked that :

"This is a secret *Nikah* and I cannot permit it. Had there been any citation of the Holy Prophet (S.A.W.) or Hazrat Abu Bakr (R.A.A.), I would have termed it an adultery and punished (the culprits) accordingly."*(Moata Imam Malik)*

Islam Prohibits Prostitution

Prostitution is totally prohibited in Islam. Before its advent, the ignorant Arabs had opened centres of prostitution for the public. The rich men generally forced their maid servants to practise prostitution for the benefit of their masters. The advent of Islam put a total ban for ever on this unnatural and unlawful trade of prostitution. The Holy Quran says :

"But force not your maids for prostitution, if they desire to lead a pious life." (24 : 33)

Very often, the master did not force his maid servant for prostitution, but would ask her to pay him a very heavy amount of money which she could not earn normally and was forced to indulge in immoral practice to earn enough money to pay her master. The Holy Prophet (S.A.W.) refused to accept this tyrannical practice of the masters and directed them to abstain from such tyrannical behaviour for the purpose of earning money. Raf'e-bin-Rafah says :

"The Holy Prophet (S.A.W.) has prohibited acceptance of the earnings of the maid-servants unless it is earned through lawful means. Then gesturing with his fingers he said, 'For instance cooking, spinning or ginning'."
(Abu Dawood)

Rafe-bin-Khadij (R.A.A.) relates, "The Holy Prophet (S.A.W.) has prohibited the acceptance of the maid-servant's earning unless it is ascertained how it is earned."
(Abu Dawood)

This *Hadis* means that only the amount of lawful earning of a maid-servant can be accepted by her master.

Before the advent of Islam the ignorant Arabs kept some special maid servants for the purpose of running the trade of prostitution. Therefore, the Quranic verses were revealed to the Holy Prophet (S.A.W.) for the eradication of this evil. The Holy Prophet (S.A.W.) himself prohibited this unlawful trade.

As the laws of Islam are meant for all times and will continue to be effective until the Day of Judgment, the prostitution remains forbidden even in this modern world. No time or place can make any modification in the laws of Islam. Hence the trade of prostitution remains forbidden for ever. Hazrat Abu Mas'ood Ansari (R.A.A.) has narrated :

"The Holy Prophet (S.A.W.) has prohibited the acceptance of the price of dog and income from prostitution."
(Bukhari and Muslim)

The words of another *Hadis* are : "The adulterer's income is dirty and unholy."

The trade of prostitution is also condemned by the Muslim scholars and jurists. Imam Ibn Taimiyah (R.A.) says:

"If a man asks his maid-servant to earn money through fornication and to spend for her needs or he himself shares her income, then curse of Allah and His Prophet (S.A.W.) be upon him. He is an evil-doer and transgressor because he has been indulging in a great sin, and is sharing the income of a prostitute. He has failed to prevent her from lewdness, hence he must be treated as legally unreliable and he must not be allowed to live in the society of the Muslims. The man of such bad character must be punished severely until he prevents his maid-servants from the evil trade. The least punishment for him is to sever all relations with him and he must not be saluted. No prayers *(Salat)* must be offered under his lead (that is, he must not be allowed to lead the prayer) provided another Imam could be had easily. He must not be allowed to give evidence nor must he be given any post. If he considers (this earning) as lawful then he is an infidel. He must be ordered to repent and give up. If he does so, it is well and good, otherwise he should be beheaded. Owing to the nature of his offence his Muslim heirs cannot inherit his wealth or property. If he is ignorant of the law, he must be explained the law thoroughly (then only he will be dealt as mentioned above). Because, this is such an act that there is consensus of the entire *Ummah.*" *(Fatawa Ibn Taimiyah)*

Inter-mixing of Males and Females Prohibited

Inter-mixing of men and women is not allowed in an Islamic society, whereas all other societies have permitted the free intermixing of the two sexes. Unless this practice is done away with, no society can remain free from the social evils.

Islam has limited intermixing with the blood relations only and prohibited the general intermixing of men and women at any place. Hardly any occasion comes when men and women could have an opportunity to get together on the basis of the principles of Islam. Even if men and women have to work in a common place, they should remain separate from one another. Abdullah bin 'Umar (R.A.A.) has related that the Holy Prophet (S.A.W.) has prohibited a woman from walking between two men. *(Abu Dawood)*

Once the Holy Prophet (S.A.W.) observed men and women mixing with one another and ordered the women, "Move back because you have no right to occupy the middle of the road. You should walk on one side of the road."

(Abu Dawood)

Consequently, the women walked so cautiously alongside the wall that their clothes got stuck to the wall."

(Abu Dawood)

Hazrat Ali (R.A.A.) says, "Are you not ashamed? I have an information that your women go to the markets where they have to face the infidels." *(Musnad Ahmad)*

Once Hazrat 'Umar Farooq (R.A.A.) was patrolling the market. He saw a man busy talking to a woman. He started whipping him. In the meanwhile, the person said, "*Ameerul Momineen*, she is my wife." Hazrat 'Umar (R.A.A.) was very sorry to hear this and said, "I am very sorry for having whipped you. You can avenge if you wish." He replied, "I have pardoned you." *(Al'Aqd-ul-Fareed)*

Not only that Islam prohibits the mixing of men and women, but also the going out of the women adorned in attractive dress and thus spreading the germs of evil in the society. Hazrat Abu Moosa (R.A.A.) relates that the Holy Prophet (S.A.W.) has said, "Every eye commits adultery (therefore, women should pass unseen by men). If a woman applies strong perfume and passes through a group of men then she is such and such woman, that is she is an adultress."

(Tirmizi)

Hazrat Abu Hurairah has related that the Holy Prophet (S.A.W.) has said, "A woman who uses perfume, should not offer the Isha prayers with us (in the mosque)."

(Abu Dawood)

Imam Navavi (R.A.A.) says, "On the basis of the *Ahadis*, the scholars maintain that a woman can be permitted to go to the mosque provided she has not applied perfume, has not adorned herself, has not wore the *pazeb* (ornament of the feet giving tinkling sound) which could be heard, she has not worn gaudy dress, she has not mixed up with males, she is not young or in such a state that she may create trouble or there should be any fear of disturbance." *(Sharh Muslim)*

Allama Ibn Ilham Hanafi says, "When we say that woman is allowed to leave home, then this is done on the condition that she would not adorn herself nor should she be in a state that may attract attention of men." *(Fath-ul-Qadeer)*

Imam Ibn Qayyim (R.A.) says, "It is incumbent upon the ruler to prevent the mixing up of men and women in the markets, the open places and in the assembly of men because he is accountable to Allah in this respect. It is a big evil and to prevent evil is the duty of the ruler. The Holy Prophet (S.A.W.) has said, "I have left behind no greater mischief than women for men." According to another *Hadis*, the Holy Prophet (S.A.W.) has said to the women, "You should walk by the side of the road." It is also the duty of the ruler to prevent women from going out (of their homes) well adorned. He must not allow her to go out in such dresses in which she appears to be naked, for instance loose and thin dress. It is also his duty to prevent men and women talking to one another on the roads. Some jurists opine that if a woman goes out fully adorned, the ruler has the right to spoil her clothes with ink, etc. This is the least pecuniary punishment. If she happens to go out (without reason), specially wearing guady clothes, then the ruler has the right to imprison her and if he leaves her unpunished, it would amount to his abetment of her evil act. Hazrat 'Umar Farooq (R.A.A.) had prohibited women from walking on the path which is meant for men, that is, walking in the middle of the road. It is incumbent upon the ruler to follow the example set by Hazrat 'Umar Farooq (R.A.A.)."

(At turqi-Hikmiya-Fis-Siasat-ul-Shariah)

Vulgarity not Allowed

Pornography is also a great menace for the society. Leading of virtuous life can be possible only if the root cause that spreads evil in the society is eliminated and its publicity banned. It is not possible for the people to keep off from the evil, when the educational institutions are devoid of the concept of good morals and the radio, T.V., newspaper, and magazines are busy in publishing the obscene material.

Before the advent of Islam, the Arabian society was notoriously known for its free and unbridled sex. The poets incited the sexual instinct through their compositions, the writers described different forms of sexual acts in such vulgar language that decent people could not dare repeat those works. Islam declared that publicity of vulgarity is a very serious crime which cannot be tolerated in the Islamic society at any cost. The Holy Quran says :

> "Those who love (to see) scandal publish, broadcast among the believers, will have a grievous penalty in the life and the Hereafter : Allah knows and ye know not."
>
> (24 : 19)

'Ata, an associate of the companions says, "One who spreads shamelessness, shall be awarded exemplary punishment, although he may be speaking the truth."

(Al Mohilla, Ibn Hazm)

Some people try to paint the picture of lawful relations in such a manner that excite the human passions. The Holy Prophet (S.A.W.) has prohibited this. He (S.A.W.) says, "The worst place will be of that man who has slept with his wife and spread its secrecy." *(Muslim)*

Once the Holy Prophet (S.A.W.) asked the audience after the prayers, "Do you draw curtain and close the doors when you have sexual relation with your wife?" The people replied "Yes." Then again the Holy Prophet (S.A.W.) asked, "Do you not talk about it publicly?" The people kept quiet. The same question he (S.A.W.) asked from a group of the women. They also kept quiet. But a young girl got up and said, "O Messenger of Allah (S.A.W.), yes, all the men and the women talk about such affairs." After hearing the reply of the girl, the Holy Prophet (S.A.W.) said, "Do you know what does this mean? It is like a male Satan meeting a female Satan in a street and there he starts having sex with her before the people. Remember, the publicity of vulgarity is made in different ways; even through adornment. The scent of the man is that, the perfume of which remains apparent but the colour remains hidden and for the women, the perfume should be such that its colour be visible but not the fragrance." *(Abu Dawood)*.

Ta'zeer (Punishment)

Even if, after all such reformatory measures, any individual or party tries to obstruct the way of piety, Islam uses its full force to curb such evil. It never allows any effort to succeed in the spreading of evil. There were such people, during the time of the Holy Prophet (S.A.W.), who never liked to see the society free from all vices. They always strived to spoil it. The Holy Quran warned such people and commanded to desist from such nefarious designs else they would be punished very severely.

The Holy Quran says :

> "Truly, if the hypocrites and those with diseased hearts and mischief mongers who try to create disturbance in the city, do not desist from nefarious activities, shall be placed under you (Muhammad S.A.W.) and will be expelled from Madina. They shall have a curse on them; wherever they are found, they shall be seized and slain (without mercy)." (33 : 60-61)

Hazrat 'Umar Farooq (R.A.A.) had sent in exile such men who tried to spoil the society by their evil deeds. There was a man named Jadat-us-Salma. His habit was to take the women out of the city and talk to them when the *Mujahideen* were out on the battlefield. ***(Fath-ul-Bari)***. When the *Mujahidden* came to know of this fact, they wrote to Hazrat 'Umar Farooq (R.A.A.), who at once drove him out of Madina.

Once, Hazrat 'Umar Farooq (R.A.A.) was on night patrol. He heard a woman reciting this couplet :

"Is there any possibility of getting wine and embracing Nasr-bin-Hajjaj."

The next day Hazrat 'Umar Farooq (R.A.A.) sent for Nasr bin Hajjaj. He looked to be a very handsome man. Hazrat 'Umar Farooq (R.A.A.) asked him to dress his hair. When he did this his charm was further enhanced. Then Hazrat 'Umar Farooq (R.A.A.) asked him to put on his turban. When he put on his turban he became more attractive. Hazrat 'Umar Farooq concluded that the restlessness and the earnest desire of the woman last night showed that she had developed illicit relations with Nasr-bin-Hajjaj. Therefore, Hazrat 'Umar made necessary arrangement for his journey to Basrah. Because, his presence in Madina might have created chances for evil practices. *(Al Isaba)*

A eunuch in emergencies used to visit private houses freely. Once he was heard saying to Abdullah, the brother of Hazrat Umme Salama (R.A.A.), "If Taif is conquered, I shall show you such and such pretty (woman). Then he described the beauty of that woman in such a manner that showed that he still had sexual feelings. By chance, the Holy Prophet (S.A.W.) heard him. The Holy Prophet (S.A.W.), therefore, asked his wives not to allow him to enter their houses. And according to another version, he was sent away to the desert outside Madina.

(Bukhari, Muslim and Abu Dawood)

Hazrat 'Umar Farooq (R.A.A.) had also exiled a eunuch. It is also related that Hazrat Abu Bakr (R.A.A.) also took such action. *(Bukhari and Behaqi)*

Islamic Punishment

There are two types of punishments for sexual crimes : *Rajm* (Stoning to death) and lashing. These punishments are given in the extreme cases of sexual crimes.

The men who indulges in bawdy talks are exiled under Islamic law; and those who even after having lawful means for the fulfilment of their sexual desires commit adultery are lashed. And those who are married and have the lawful means to satisfy their sexual wants and yet indulge in fornication, have no right to exist on the earth. They are to be wiped out in order to keep the society clean. The Holy Quran says :

> "The woman and the man guilty of adultery or fornication are to be flogged with a hundered stripes each; let no compassion move you in their case (to show leniency) in a matter prescribed by Allah, if ye believe in Allah and the Day of Judgment. And let a party of believers witness their punishment." (24 : 2)

Explaining the above verse of the Holy Quran, the Holy Prophet (S.A.W.) says that this commandment is for the unmarried men and women. And one who commits adultery after marriage, would be stoned to death. Ubadah bin Samit (R.A.A.) relates that the Holy Prophet (S.A.W.) has said :

"Lo'! listen to my orders : Lo! Listen to my orders. Allah has determined the punishment for the adultress. If a virgin commits adultery with a bachelor, both must be lashed one hundred stripes, and shall be exiled for one year. If a married woman commits adultery with a married man both shall be awarded one hundred lashes and stoned to death."
(Muslim)

On the basis of this *Hadis*, Imam Ahmad (R.A.), Ishaque (R.A.) and Dawood (R.A.) say that if a married man commits adultery, first he shall be lashed and then stoned to death. But Imam Abu Hanifa (R.A.), Abu Yusuf (R.A.), Zufar (R.A.), Muhammad (R.A.), Imam Shafie (R.A.) Imam Malik (R.A.) Ibne Abi Laila, Auzayee (R.A.) Sauri (R.A.) and Hassan bin Saleh (R.A.) opine that there shall be no lashing along with the punishment of *Rajm*.

If an unmarried man is found guilty of adultery, he shall be awarded one hundred lashes. But the jurists differ on the point of exile. Imam Shafie (R.A.) and Imam Ahmad bin Hanbal (R.A.) maintain that an adulterer, whether man or woman, who is unmarried must be awarded lashes and also exiled for one year. But Imam Shafie (R.A.) maintains that if an adulterer is a slave, he shall be exiled only for six months.

Imam Malik (R.A.) and Imam Auzayee (R.A.) says that the punishment of exile shall be awarded to men only and not to women. The Hanafi jurists do not consider the punishment of exile a part of the *hud*. They maintain that it depends on the discretion of the Imam and the prevailing circumstances. The ruler will act in the interest of the Islamic state and refrain from what is harmful to it."

(Ahkam-ul-Quran, Jassas)

There are two important objects of the exile : The one is to make the conditions unfavourable to the accused and remove him from the place where he has the chances of committing wrong, otherwise it will be difficult to save him from the offence. The second aim is to provide the accused an opportunity to mend his ways and become good. When he is away from his homeland, he may lose his sexual appetite. In the alien land he has to struggle for his survival, therefore, he has no time to think of his unlawful sexual desire.

These detailed discussions prove that the fulfilment of unlawful sexual desire is forbidden in Islam and that the only allowed course is lawful means, that is, the man and the woman must marry according to the Islamic *Shariah* for gratifying their sexual desire. A person who crosses the limits laid down by the Holy Quran, has to face the punishment prescribed by it.

Islam wants that the human wants must be satisfied but these wants must be natural and in accordance with the commandments of Allah and the practices of the Holy Prophet (S.A.W.). It also expects the Islamic State to provide all facilities in respect of the marriage of the Muslim men and women.

The aim of Islam is to regularise the human activities in accordance with the Holy Quran and the *Sunnah*. It forbids all unnatural and unlawful activities because it is the only way to eradicate evil from the human society. Hence, if the world wants real peace and happiness, it must adopt the principles of the Holy Quran and the *Sunnah*. And Islam alone has given the honourable status to women in the human society and also granted them equal rights according to their natural requirements and human needs. There is no discrimination on the basis of sex in Islam. Hence Islam is the only means of salvation for the entire mankind.

==*=*=*=*=*